A Lover's Pursuit

Giving Your Heart
to Allah (s.w.t) and
His Messenger (s.a.w)

WAEL IBRAHIM
MUFTI ISMAIL MENK
DR MUHAMMAD SALAH

Published by:

TERTIB
PUBLISHING

Unit No. E-10-5, Jalan SS 15/4G, Subang Square,
47500 Subang Jaya, Selangor, Malaysia
+603-5612-2407 (office) / +6017-399-7411 (mobile)
info@tertib.press
www.tertib.press
@tertibpress (Facebook & Instagram)

Author	:	Wael Ibrahim
		Mufti Ismail Menk
		Dr Muhammad Salah
Editor / transcriber:		Nadiah Aslam
		Norashikin Azizan
		Arisha Mohd Affendy
Cover designer	:	Abdul Adzim Md Daim
Typesetter	:	Abdul Adzim Md Daim

A LOVER'S PURSUIT:
GIVING YOUR HEART TO ALLAH (S.W.T)
AND HIS MESSENGER (S.A.W)

First Edition: December 2023

Perpustakaan Negara Malaysia

Cataloguing-in-Publication Data

A catalogue record for this book is available from the National Library of Malaysia

ISBN: 978-967-2844-32-7 (hardback)

Table of Contents

Introduction 1

Editor's Note 2

Summary and Overview 3

Ending remarks 5

The Soul and The Self
Wael Ibrahim 6

Muhammad and Me
Mufti Ismail Menk 48

Allah and I
Dr Muhammad Salah 112

Questions & Answers 159

Arabic Glossary 187

Introduction

All praises due to Allah and all praises to Him as we seek His help and guidance. Whoever Allah guides is the truly guided ones, and whoever Allah leads astray, none can show him guidance. May the greatest peace and blessings be upon Prophet Muḥammad (s.a.w.).

In the symphony of gratitude, let our hearts resonate with *Alḥamdulillāh wa kafa*, seeking the melody of divine connection. As the echoes of *salam* dance through the air, we embark on a profound exploration—A Lover's Pursuit, where hearts intertwine with the essence of Allah and His Messenger.

Picture this: a tapestry woven with praises to the Almighty, a tale where guidance is a compass leading to the truest of loves. May the profound peace and blessings bestowed upon Prophet Muḥammad (s.a.w.) be our guiding star in this celestial narrative.

Today, we unravel the layers of affection, dissecting the anatomy of genuine love for the sake of Allah. For, in the tapestry of existence, to love Allah is to embrace the entirety of creation. As we traverse the corridors of this transcribed symposium, The Faith Conference of May 20, 2023, titled *A Lover's Pursuit: Giving Your Heart to Allah (s.w.t) and His Messenger (s.a.w.)*, anticipate a profound revelation, a resourceful insight into the very fabric of true love.

Take this journey with Dr. Muhammad Salah as he imparts the art of loving Allah in *Allah and I*; traverses the intimate connection with the Prophet (s.a.w.) alongside Mufti Menk in *Muḥammad and Me*, and explore self-appreciation through the lens of Shaykh Wael Ibrahim in *The Soul and the Self*.

In the tapestry of words laid before you, may you *inshā'Allāh*, find not just knowledge but a tranquil sanctuary where the intricate dance of these ideas unfolds into a melody of wisdom. As we delve into the heart of devotion, may these words be a compass guiding us toward benefits and serenity.

Let the journey into the depths of love begin.

Editor's Note

Do you know what true love is?

Allah (s.w.t.) is true love.
He is the foundation of love.

All the love, affection and compassion that you feel and see are from Allah. The people who love you, the warmth from strangers, the affection of animals, and the blessings and challenges that you have are all due to Allah's love for us.

When you love Allah, it will guide you to love people and things for His sake. And so, when you love Allah, undeniably you will come to love His Messenger (s.a.w.) as well. Consequently, when you embark on a journey of loving Allah and His Messenger (s.a.w.), you will discover ways to love yourself correctly too. You will uncover the wondrous ways to love yourself in the way Islam has proclaimed. You will learn to treat yourself delicately and not as how society portrays self-love.

With that, Tertib Publishing has decided to be your companion on this journey by presenting to you a never-before-seen 3-in-1 book collection for your quest. This remarkable book titled *A Lover's Pursuit* has been transcribed and meticulously edited based on the conference conducted by Faith Events in May 2023 with the same title.

Under the same umbrella theme of pursuing love, three notable speakers—Dr Muhammad Salah, Wael Ibrahim, and Mufti Menk—give us profound insight from different lenses for this quest.

Summary and Overview

In this book, we cover the following topics that all fall under the same umbrella theme of *A Lover's Pursuit.*

1. **The Soul and The Self**

   By Wael Ibrahim

   In the first section, Shaykh Wael beckons on how self-love is a part of our beautiful religion. The portrayal of self-love in our current society and social media is minuscule compared to Islam. Hence, the speaker dives into many meanings of self-love in Islam, allowing us to discover that true self-love is selfless. Self-love in the lenses of Islam will elevate our status and bring us closer to our Creator, Allah. Not only that, this section implores us to remember our self-worth which is being the creation of Allah Almighty; a creation that Allah has honoured and dignified.

2. **Muhammad and Me**

   By Mufti Menk

   In the second section, we venture into the journey of our beloved Prophet's love for his *ummah* and his sacrifices. Exploring and focusing on the extraordinary aspects of the Prophet's life, the section discusses his perfect creation, his illumination like the moon, and the miracles and blessings in nature that connect people with him. It also addresses the challenge of balancing spirituality with modern comforts. By knowing the greatest creation, you will love Allah as you follow his (s.a.w.) footsteps and practise the *din* just like he did.

3. **Allah and I**

   By Dr Muhammad Salah

   Allah and I showcases various significant lessons of His remarkable servants since the companion's period; a lesson to remember and indulge in to become a Muslim that will be loved by Allah (s.w.t.). Learning and adopting the qualities and traits that Allah (s.w.t.) loves such as loving one another for His sake is one of the means to seeking

His love. In addition, this section illustrates the way Allah loves His servants, as well as gently reminding us that when we are loved by Allah, we will be put under His shade on the Day of Judgement.

Ending this profound pursuit of love is the Questions and Answers section that was conducted during the conference among the three speakers. The interactive session enabled the audience to pose their unanswered questions which were clarified and answered by our esteemed speakers.

Ending remarks

On a side note, Tertib's Editorial Team would like to highlight that, *alḥamdulillāh,* this book has been edited from scratch to make it suitable for readers from different walks of life. In order to improve the readability of the book, the content was polished and restructured. In addition, each speaker's style was retained to preserve the authenticity.

Dear reader, before you turn the helm over to the next page and ride off into the sunset to chase the pursuit of love, we pray that this knowledge will be beneficial to you in this life and the next. May the knowledge that you gain be put into practice bit by bit, and may Allah accept all of your deeds. *Āmīn*

Tertib Publishing.

Table of Contents

Preface **9**

Chapter 1: Self-love for starters **11**
What is self-love? 12
Self-love VS Narcissistic Love 14
Self-love is a natural human trait 16

Chapter 2: Self-love in the lenses of Islam **18**
Self-care 19
Selfless 27
Self-worth 29

Chapter 3: Self-Love as a Way of Life **31**
Loving Others 32
Honesty and Truthfulness 35
Authentic 37
Confidence 41
Contentment 42
Tranquillity 43

Chapter 4: Conclusion **45**

The Soul and The Self

Wael Ibrahim

Preface

In the chaotic journey of our modern lives, where the noise of self-doubt and societal expectations often drowns the whispers of the soul, the concept of self-love emerges as a beacon of clarity and yet an often misunderstood facet of our existence. And so, I would like to welcome you all to a journey that transcends the superficial notions of self-care propagated by the world around us. In the pages that follow, we explore the profound depth of self-love through the lens of our beautiful religion—Islam, navigating the intricate balance between self-worth and humility, and finding solace in the authentic teachings of our faith and the authenticity of who we really are.

Within the richness of Islam, the idea of self-love is not merely an indulgence in the superficial or a fleeting emotion dictated by the ever-changing tides of the world. Instead, it is a journey inward, guided by the divine light of Allah's wisdom and the timeless teachings of our beloved Prophet Muḥammad (s.a.w).

From the very core of our faith emerges the acknowledgement of the intrinsic value of the self. The Qur'an itself speaks to the sanctity of human life:

"And We have certainly honoured the children of Adam…"

(Surah al-Isra', 17:70)

In this honour lies an invitation—a call to recognise and appreciate the sanctity of our own existence, viewing ourselves through the lens of an ultimate Divine Love.

Our beloved Prophet Muḥammad (s.a.w.), in his profound wisdom, reminded us of the importance of self-care—not as a selfish pursuit, but as a means to honour the gift of life bestowed upon us by our Creator. He (s.a.w.) said in a hadith:

"...your body has a right over you…"

(Ṣaḥiḥ al-Bukhari 6134)

The statement resonates as a gentle reminder that self-love is a duty—a responsibility to care for the vessel through which we navigate this worldly journey.

Yet, this journey into self-love is not a solitary one. Islam beautifully intertwines the love of self with the love of others, encouraging a harmonious balance between self-care and selflessness.

The Prophet (s.a.w.) also emphasised,

> "None of you will have faith till he wishes for his (Muslim) brother what he likes for himself."
>
> (Ṣaḥiḥ al-Bukhari 13)

In this profound statement lies the interconnectedness of our individual well-being with the well-being of those around us.

As we embark on this exploration, let us remember that self-love in Islam is not a licence for arrogance or narcissism. The Prophet (s.a.w.) cautioned against the weight of pride in our hearts, as

> "He who has in his heart the weight of a mustard seed of pride shall not enter Paradise…"
>
> (Ṣaḥiḥ Muslim 91a)

So, join me, dear readers, brothers and sisters, on this spiritual experience—a journey into the heart of self-love, guided by the divine compass of Islam.

May this exploration deepen our connection with Allah (s.w.t), illuminate our understanding of self, and inspire a profound transformation that echoes through the chambers of our souls. *Āmīn.*

Love you all for the sake of Allah.

Wael Ibrahim

Chapter 1

Self-love for starters

Alḥamdulillāh all praise due to Allah (s.w.t.) who has granted me the opportunity to talk about this topic. Before we dive into the book bi iznillāh, please filter your intentions my dear brothers and sisters—which is to gain knowledge only for the sake of Allah (s.w.t.).

What is self-love?

How many of us have heard the word self-love in the past couple of years? Many of us have definitely heard the word "self-love" and statements regarding it.

A few years ago, I was invited to a workshop. The course was titled "Self-care, Self-love for Counsellors." As someone who is working in the field and profession of counselling, I decided to attend the course to increase and add more knowledge for myself. After the meet and greet session at the workshop, the instructor went up to the stage and started asking the audience a few questions.

One of the questions that he asked was, "When was the last time you woke up in the morning and decided to head to the bathroom to prepare yourself a bubble bath?" For an Egyptian like me, saying the words "bubble bath" was very difficult. It even sounds disgusting to me. Some people raised their hands to the question but the majority did not. I mean who does that you know, prepare themselves a bubble bath? The instructor proceeds to ask another question. He asked the audience, "How often do you go for massages?" He then shouted for the ladies in the room and asked, "Ladies, how many times have you called your husband to tell him that you won't be cooking for the day and instead will be going to the spa?" The instructor had a long list of questions however I just want to mention a few. My favourite question of them all was when he asked the audience "Do you wake up every morning heading straight to the mirror to look at yourself and say I Love You?"

That was it for me. I left the room immediately. Before leaving, the instructor concluded his long list of questions by saying "This my friends is self-love." *Allāhu Akbar.* This poor soul, this poor man, did not actually know that *alḥamdulillāh* for us Muslims, bathing and showering is **absolutely** normal. It is normal. It is not a sign of either hate or love. It is just a part of our existence. The Prophet (s.a.w.) said in the following hadith:

...الطُّهُورُ شَطْرُ الإِيمَانِ...

Cleanliness is half of faith

(Ṣaḥiḥ Muslim 223)

Cleanliness, purity, or purifying ourselves is half of our *iman*—half of our faith. *Allāhu Akbar*. Our *mashaikh*, our scholars have reflected on this. The scholars questioned and wondered how the substance water—the symbol of purity and cleanliness constitutes half of our *iman*. The scholars said later that it is because we have in our religion the ritualistic act of worship called *wuḍu'*. What is the preparation of *wuḍu'* for? It is for *ṣalah*. What is *ṣalah*? The main foundation of the *din*. The Prophet (s.a.w.) mentioned the following:

الصَّلَاةُ لِوَقْتِهَا، وَمَنْ تَرَكَ الصَّلَاةَ فَلَا دِينَ لَهُ، وَالصَّلَاةُ عِمَادُ الدِّينِ

> Praying on time, whoever leaves the prayer then there is no religion for him and the prayer is the pillar of religion.
>
> (al-Bayhaqi 2550, Syuʿab al-iman)

Ṣalah is the main pillar—the main foundation of the *din*. Prayer is a pillar of the religion, Islam. Whosoever establishes that pillar and makes it firm, has established the entire *din*. Thus, the *ṭaharah* or purification comprises half of our *iman*. *SubḥānAllāh*.

One thing that we should remember my brothers and sisters in Islam, is that the concept of self-love as told by social media—Twitter, Facebook, and Instagram is limited. In general, the entertainment industry and social media teach that self-love is about cleaning yourself. Hence, making self-love very limited to that category. For instance, going to the spa, going for massages, manicures, and pedicures. All these examples can actually be a good thing that we can include as part of the package of being a Muslim.

There is no problem in doing it, so long as you are doing it for the right reason. You are doing it for your husband or wife, or yourself. As long as you don't display your beauty to strangers and so on, it is alright in Islam. However, this is just a very tiny, teeny aspect of self-love described in our beautiful religion. Thus, I will be *inshā'Allāh* focusing on this topic in the upcoming chapters as well.

Self-love VS Narcissistic Love

A very important note before we delve further into the topic:

I would like to highlight that when I use the term self-love, I will not be referring to something in Arabic called *al-ʿujub* or *al-ʿajab*. *Al-ʿujub* is excessive self-admiration whereby you love yourself too much to the point of not liking anyone else or not even considering anyone else. It is a narcissistic kind of love. I am not referring to that kind of love because that kind of self-love is actually a disease that could lead us to one of the greatest sins—*kibr*. What is *kibr*? It is arrogance. Be careful with arrogance my dear brothers and sisters.

What did the Prophet (s.a.w.) say about arrogance? The Prophet (s.a.w.) said:

> He who has in his heart the weight of a mustard seed of pride shall not enter Paradise. A person (amongst his hearers) said: Verily a person loves that his dress should be fine, and his shoes should be fine. He (the Holy Prophet) remarked: Verily, Allah is Graceful and He loves Grace. Pride is disdaining the truth (out of self-conceit) and contempt for the people.
>
> (Ṣaḥiḥ Muslim 91a)

This hadith begins with the following statement: "He will not enter *Jannah*."

Can you imagine the Prophet (s.a.w.) beginning his words by making a declaration that "such and such will **not** enter *Jannah*"? The Prophet (s.a.w.) describes in the hadith above that the person who will not enter *Jannah* is whomsoever who has an atom weight of a master seed of arrogance in his heart, *walā ʾaʿūdhubillāh*. A person who has arrogance will not enter *Jannah*. May Allah protect us all, *amīn*.

The hadith then continues with questions from the companions. Some of the companions asked, "O' Messenger of Allah, some of us love to dress nicely." Basically, some of the companions love to dress nicely—they like to wear nice clothes and shoes. They asked that question as they wondered if it was permissible in the religion. The Prophet (s.a.w.) responded and said

"Allah is beautiful and He loves beauty." What does this statement mean? It means taking care of your outer appearance is not haram. In fact, it is actually a part of self-love—a part of Islam. Taking care of your outer appearance does not mean that you are arrogant.

The Prophet (s.a.w.) further defines in the hadith to the companions the two meanings of *kibr*. The first definition of *kibr* is *batarul haqq*. What is *batarul haqq*? It is to know the truth and reject it; to admit within yourself the truth and reject it. For instance, when a brother or a sister is advising you to put the hijab on nicely, you know for a fact that it is the truth but you reject it— as you don't want to accept the truth. And so, that is arrogance, *walā ʾaʿūdhubillāh.*

The second definition of *kibr* is to look down upon people—to think that you are higher than others. These two definitions are what *kibr* is about. On the other hand, taking care of your outer appearance is absolutely acceptable in Islam.

Self-love is a natural human trait

I want to remind you my dear readers of a very interesting fact which is by nature we all love ourselves. What do you think? Is it true or false?

My dear brothers and sisters, have you seen yourselves taking selfies of yourself? Like have you seen someone opening their camera all of a sudden in metro stations or restaurants and then taking a selfie with a pretty pose? **That is loving yourself.** Can you see how selfish a selfie is? It is called a selfie for a reason. You are posing for yourself. You are posing in front of people **but** it is actually just for yourself. You pose just for yourself. You love yourself so much that you take a picture of yourself.

I want you to do an experiment my dear readers with your family and friends. At least five people should be involved in this experiment. What you have to do in this experiment is basically take a selfie with five people. After you have snapped the selfie look at it. Focus and look at the picture.

Now, my question is who did you first look at in the selfie? Which person did you look at first in the selfie? **Definitely yourself**.

Editors note

This interesting experiment was conducted during the lecture as well. Five brothers were called up to the front to take a selfie. After the selfie was captured, all the brothers looked at it. Shaykh Wael then proceeds to ask one of the brothers "Who did you look at first in the picture?" The brother answered, ***"myself".***

#Experiment has proven to be a success

#We love ourselves naturally

#Selfie is selfish

The experiment will show you that we really do love ourselves naturally. You will most definitely look at yourself first and foremost in the selfie. That is what a selfie does to you. It's ME, I and NOBODY ELSE. Nobody in the picture matters except you. *SubḥānAllāh.* However, this is our human nature. We want to look the best; we want to be the best and that is OK to an extent because Allah (s.w.t.) says to us in the Qur'an:

قَدْ أَفْلَحَ مَن تَزَكَّىٰ ﴿١٤﴾

He has certainly succeeded who purifies himself

(Surah al-A'la, 87:14)

Who is this successful person?

It is the one who purifies himself—the one who purifies his soul. And so, because of this understanding within our religion, within our system, within ourselves, we thus need to look at ourselves from time to time to modify ourselves. We need to look back at ourselves in order to modify and design ourselves in that matter.

Chapter 2

Self-love in the lenses of Islam

In this chapter, I will be defining self-love from the perspective of Islam. There are three. The first is taking care of yourself, the second is loving others and the third increasing your self-worth.

Self-care

Self-love is looking after yourself in four areas:

- 🧡 *Physically*
- 🧡 *Mentally*
- 🧡 *Emotionally*
- 🧡 *Spiritually*

Physically

Take care of yourself physically by wearing nice garments and shoes. If you want to have and wear a nice watch, that too is not a problem. I touched upon this in the previous chapter as well:

> He who has in his heart the weight of a mustard seed of pride shall not enter Paradise. A person (amongst his hearers) said: Verily a person loves that his dress should be fine, and his shoes should be fine. He (the Holy Prophet) remarked: Verily, Allah is Graceful and He loves Grace. Pride is disdaining the truth (out of self-conceit) and contempt for the people.
>
> (Ṣaḥiḥ Muslim 91a)

Allah is beautiful and He loves beauty.

So, beautify yourselves, my dear brothers and sisters. There is no problem as long as you do for the right reasons. At the same time, remember to do the same thing mentally as well.

Mentally

Remember to look after yourself mentally. Do you know the entire story of Prophet Muḥammad's encounter with Jibra'il (a.s.) in the cave of Hira'—

Jabal an-Nur? Did the Prophet (s.a.w.) see Jibra'il (a.s.) in his actual form? Is this statement true or false? This is a true statement.

Do you know how Jibra'il (a.s.) looks like? He is an angel with 600 wings. This description of the angel Jibra'il (a.s.) was narrated by the Prophet (s.a.w.) himself. The Prophet (s.a.w.) even mentioned that if 1 of his 600 wings were to spread, it would block the sunlight from reaching the earth.

Narrated Ash-Sha'bi:

> ...Rather he (s.a.w.) saw Jibra'il, but he did not see him in his (real) image except two times. One time at *Sidrat Al-Muntaha* and one time in *Jiyad*, he had six hundred wings which filled the horizon.
>
> (Jami' at-Tirmidhi 3278)

It was narrated that 'Abdullah (r.a.) said:

> The Messenger of Allah (s.a.w.) saw Jibra'il in his true form: he has six hundred wings, each of which fills the horizon and there falls from his wings things of different colours, pearls and rubies of which Allah knows best.
>
> (Musnad Aḥmad 3748)

Imagine now a similar figure appearing before you. How will you behave when such a thing happens? How do you think you will react? How many of you are into horror movies my dear readers? I know a lot of people are. People just love watching horror movies. *Allāhu Akbar.*

Imagine now: You are watching a horror movie while knowing that it is scripted. At the same time, you do know that something is going to pop up and scare you. And now when the scary, terrifying part comes, what happens? You get scared. *Allāhu Akbar.* Honestly my dear readers if it's not you who watches, then ask your friend who loves horror movies. Ask them as well, why they don't visit the toilet in the middle of the movie. It is definitely because they are afraid that the scary figure will come to them in the bathroom.

Back to the Prophet Muḥammad (s.a.w.) and Jibra'il's encounter. Imagine now, the Prophet (s.a.w.) seeing a huge figure, an angel with might—with 600 wings and one of the wings is capable of blocking the sunlight from reaching the earth. During the encounter at the Cave of Hira', the angel, Jibra'il (a.s.) conversed with the Prophet (s.a.w.). "Read" Jibra'il (a.s.) had commanded to the Prophet Muḥammad (s.a.w.). Not only that, Jibra'il (a.s.) also hugged the Prophet (s.a.w.) three times. The Prophet (s.a.w.) mentioned that every time the angel hugged him, he felt distressed. He (s.a.w.) thought that his ribs would pop out of his body. That was how severe the experience was.

What did the Prophet (s.a.w.) do after his encounter with Jibra'il (a.s.)? What did he do? The minute the angel disappeared he (s.a.w.) ran to seek comfort. From whom did he seek comfort? It was none other than Sayyidatina Khadijah (r.a.), his beloved wife. What did the Prophet (s.a.w.) tell her? What was his first statement to her? "Cover me." The Prophet (s.a.w.) also told her that he (s.a.w.) was afraid that something bad might happen to him. He (s.a.w.) felt as if a *jinn* had possessed him.

Narrated 'A'isyah (r.a.):

> …till one day he received the Guidance while he was in the cave of Hira'. An Angel came to him and asked him to read. Allah's Messenger (s.a.w.) replied, "I do not know how to read." The Prophet (s.a.w.) added, "Then the Angel held me (forcibly) and pressed me so hard that I felt distressed. Then he released me and again asked me to read, and I replied, 'I do not know how to read.' Thereupon he held me again and pressed me for the second time till I felt distressed. He then released me and asked me to read, but again I replied. 'I do not know how to read.' Thereupon he held me for the third time and pressed me till I got distressed, and then he released me and said, 'Read, in the Name of your Lord Who has created (all that exists), has created man out of a clot, Read! And your Lord is the Most Generous. Who has taught (the writing) by the pen, has taught man that which he knew not." (96.1-5). Then Allah's Messenger (s.a.w.) returned with that experience; and the muscles between his neck and shoulders were trembling till he came upon Khadijah (his wife) and said, "Cover me!" They covered him, and when the state of fear was over, he said to Khadijah, "O' Khadijah! What is wrong with me? I was afraid that

> something bad might happen to me." Then he told her the story. Khadijah said, "Nay! But receive the good tidings! By Allah, Allah will never disgrace you, for by Allah, you keep good relations with your Kith and kin, speak the truth, help the poor and the destitute, entertain your guests generously and assist those who are stricken with calamities."...
>
> (Ṣaḥiḥ al-Bukhari 4953)

What does this incident tell us? It tells us that sometimes, mentally, we get disturbed. As we experience traumatic events in our lives, we are disturbed mentally and Prophet Muḥammad (s.a.w.) was not spared from this as well. However, the Prophet (s.a.w.) did something very important, he did a crucial thing and that is seeking comfort. The Prophet (s.a.w.) sought comfort instead of fighting the traumatic experience by himself. So you can see that Islam caters for that part. *Alḥamdulillāh,* we have a religion that is absolutely comprehensive. That is why I always say don't try to seek out help from elsewhere other than our religion because *alḥamdulillāh* we have it all. *Allāhumma lakal ḥamd.*

The exception for help is when it comes to fields that require other people. For instance, medicine and so on. There is no problem in seeking help from the ones who are knowledged in that field.

Emotionally

My dear brothers and sisters in Islam, I have a question for you. How many times have you cried in front of someone and apologised for doing so? Do you have that habit of crying and then saying sorry about it?

"I'm sorry for crying."

What are you sorry for? Why are you saying sorry about your tears? Is it because you don't want the other person to feel bad? But then what about yourself?

The Prophet (s.a.w.) never apologised when he cried. In fact, when his son Ibrahim (r.a.) died, he (s.a.w.) cried. While he was burying his son, he was not only crying; the companions saw the Prophet's beard flowing with tears. His tears were flowing from between his beards and filling the ground beneath his feet with water. The companions saw this. They saw the Prophet (s.a.w.) crying. They saw the Prophet (s.a.w.) broadcasting his tears. He (s.a.w) was **telling** everyone that he was crying despite the fact that they could **see** him crying. This is how the Prophet Muḥammad (s.a.w.) used to cope with emotional and intense feelings. What did the Prophet (s.a.w.) tell the companions? It is mentioned in the following hadith:

Narrated Anas bin Malik:

> We went with Allah's Messenger (s.a.w.) to the blacksmith Abu Saif, and he was the husband of the wet nurse of Ibrahim (the son of the Prophet). Allah's Messenger (s.a.w.) took Ibrahim and kissed him and smelled him and later we entered Abu Saif's house and at that time Ibrahim was in his last breaths, and the eyes of Allah's Messenger (s.a.w.) started shedding tears. 'Abdur Rahman bin 'Auf said, "O Allah's Apostle, even you are weeping!" He said, "**O' Ibn 'Auf, this is mercy**." Then he wept more and said, "**The eyes are shedding tears and the heart is grieved, and we will not say except what pleases our Lord**, O' Ibrahim! Indeed we are grieved by your separation."
>
> (Ṣaḥiḥ al-Bukhari 1303)

The Prophet (s.a.w.) said "Indeed, my eyes are shedding tears and my heart is shattered." *Allāhu Akbar.* The intense emotions that you feel as you lose your loved ones. May Allah have mercy upon all of our family members who have passed away, *āmīn.* May Allah (s.w.t.) reunite us with them in *Jannah-al Firdaus.*

Look at the intense emotions the Prophet (s.a.w.) was going through. He (s.a.w.) wasn't ashamed to tell everyone that this is how he feels and that he needs support. At the same time, there is another important thing the Prophet (s.a.w.) said that we need to remember and focus on—more than anything else. What did the Prophet (s.a.w.) say? The Prophet (s.a.w.) said "...but we only say that which pleases Allah (s.w.t.)."

So cry all you want.

Feel your feelings all you want.

You are entitled to these emotions.

Allah (s.w.t.) created them for a reason.

The same thing with anger as well. The Prophet (s.a.w.) actually told one of his companions who sought advice to not get angry. It is mentioned in the following hadith:

Narrated Abu Hurayrah:

> A man said to the Prophet (s.a.w.), "Advise me! "The Prophet (s.a.w.) said, "Do not become angry and furious." The man asked (the same) again and again, and the Prophet (s.a.w.) said in each case, "Do not become angry and furious."
>
> (Ṣaḥiḥ al-Bukhari 6116)

The companion asked the Prophet (s.a.w.) three times for a piece of advice. And each time, the Prophet (s.a.w.) said "Don't be angry." However, this does not mean that the Prophet (s.a.w.) wanted this man to delete the emotion. "Alt+delete emotion"—to delete anger because we do not want to experience it. NO. That is nonsense. The Prophet (s.a.w.) himself became angry in many situations. What the Prophet (s.a.w.) is telling the man is to **behave in a manner that is pleasing to Allah** (s.w.t.) when he is experiencing intense emotions. The Prophet knew the man, the companion on a personal level as well as the fact that when you experience intense emotions—the internal experience of anger—you have to make sure you behave in a manner that is pleasing to Allah (s.w.t.).

The Prophet (s.a.w.) maintained his cool and calm when he was angry, however, his face would turn red. These are the description of the Prophet (s.a.w.) when he was angry based on our books of *sirah* and hadith.

> ... His face got red with anger...
>
> (Ṣaḥiḥ al-Bukhari 6109)

> ...He was bright of colour, broad of forehead, endowed with arched eyebrows, perfect without being conjoined, with a vein between them that anger would cause to pulsate...
>
> (Ash-Shama'il Al-Muḥammadiyah 8)

When the Prophet (s.a.w.) got angry, his face would turn red and a vein would appear on his forehead. He (s.a.w.) was angry. He (s.a.w.) was boiling from the inside but he never broke things; he (s.a.w.) never uttered foul language.

Do you see the difference between "deleting the emotions" and "doing what is pleasing to Allah (s.w.t.)" while experiencing and feeling the intense emotions of anger? The Prophet (s.a.w.) experienced those intense emotions of sadness and anger, and everyone is entitled to these feelings as well. So why then do we cry and say sorry? Why do we apologise for our tears? It is very weird to cry and then say sorry.

Spiritually

My dear brothers and sisters, we have to increase and improve our spirituality and look after ourselves in a spiritual manner. One of the ways is to learn more about our religion by reading and attending lectures and so on. One of our goals my dear readers should always be to take notes and learn. As you learn, have one intention in mind, that is you will put into practice what you have learned as much as you can, *inshā'Allāh.*

My dear brothers and sisters in Islam, let us be honest with ourselves for a moment. When you attend lectures and Islamic events what is your real intention? Are you coming to find peace or are you attending to see the speaker? If you are attending the lectures and events for the speaker, then it is a questionable matter. If your time, travel, money, effort, and a whole day of sitting in a lecture hall have nothing to do with an intention for Allah (s.w.t.), then you have to fix it. Our beloved Dr Muhammad Salah always reminds us about what the early *salaf* used to say that is; "It is not important who will raise the flag, who will raise the banner of victory—the banner of Islam. What is more important is for the banner to be raised by **anyone**." May Allah (s.w.t.) grant us sincerity in all that we do.

When we have improved ourselves physically, mentally, emotionally and spiritually, we have then done ourselves a favour and that is self-love. That is self-love. It's nothing about bubbles.

Selfless

Self-love is selfless. In Islam, self-love is not selfish. This is the second definition. You cannot love yourself without limits or unconditionally. Why? Because this is not in Islam. What did the Prophet (s.a.w.) say?

> Narrated Anas:
>
> The Prophet (s.a.w.) said, "None of you will have faith till he wishes for his (Muslim) brother what he likes for himself."
>
> (Ṣaḥiḥ al-Bukhari 13)

As mentioned in the above hadith, the Prophet (s.a.w.) said "None of you is a believer unless he loves for his brother or sister, what he loves for himself." Hence, you cannot just focus on yourself and leave the *dunya* behind—leave everyone else behind. Love in Islam is actually selfless. *Allāhu Akbar*. We actually have a whole lesson on something called *al-ithar*. What does *ithar* mean? Basically, it is to favour or prefer your brother or your sister's needs over your own.

At the same time, there are also small situations where the focus should be on yourself first and foremost, before others. Allah (s.w.t.) says in the Qur'an:

يَٰٓأَيُّهَا ٱلَّذِينَ ءَامَنُوا۟ قُوٓا۟ أَنفُسَكُمْ وَأَهْلِيكُمْ نَارًا وَقُودُهَا
ٱلنَّاسُ وَٱلْحِجَارَةُ عَلَيْهَا مَلَٰٓئِكَةٌ غِلَاظٌ شِدَادٌ لَّا يَعْصُونَ
ٱللَّهَ مَآ أَمَرَهُمْ وَيَفْعَلُونَ مَا يُؤْمَرُونَ ٦

> O' you who have believed, protect yourselves and your families from a Fire whose fuel is people and stones, over which are [appointed] angels, harsh and severe; they do not disobey Allah in what He commands them but do what they are commanded.
>
> (Surah at-Taḥrim, 66:6)

Allah (s.w.t.) mentions in the Qur'an to "Protect yourself and your family members from hellfire." If you are not well-equipped with the knowledge of Islam, with the knowledge of the *din*, the Qur'an, and the teaching of the Prophet (s.a.w.) first and foremost—then how will you convey this knowledge to your family? This is one of the situations where the focus should be on yourself first—whereby you need to look after yourself first by improving your knowledge and then conveying it to others. This is just one of the situations in which you should be on the frontline first.

However, when it comes to charity—when you take out from your pocket to give to others—meaning preferring others over yourself, it is self-love. *Wallāhi* that is self-love. Why? Because it will teach you **mercy**. Because it will teach you **generosity**. So, who is the one benefitting here actually? It is **you**.

Sayyidatina 'A'isyah (r.a.) used to perfume the coins for charity. Look at this beautiful act. Have we ever thought of doing this? Now though, we can't exactly perfume the money because all the charities are online. So you can't unless you want to donate money and send a perfume along with it you know. However, the main point is that she, Sayyidatina 'A'isyah (r.a.), used to **perfect** her charity. She made her charity very nice and perfect. That is why Allah (s.w.t.) says in the Qur'an:

لَن تَنَالُوا۟ ٱلْبِرَّ حَتَّىٰ تُنفِقُوا۟ مِمَّا تُحِبُّونَ ۚ ... ﴿٩٢﴾

Never will you attain the good [reward] until you spend [in the way of Allah] from that which you love...

(Surah Ali-'Imran, 3:92)

You will never attain piety and righteousness unless you spend out of that which you love the most. I have an activity that I would like you to do my dear brothers and sisters with your friends and family. It is simple. Look into your pockets or bag or purse. Take an item and give it to someone. Charity is giving from what you spend. However, for this activity, don't be too smart to the point that you take out your wallet and give it to someone—along with all your cards and IDs. Be smart. Give what you can. In a nutshell, self-love is not selfish. Self-love is selfless.

Self-worth

*Self-love in Islam is to **know your worth**.*

*Self-love in Islam is to **understand your value**.*

My dear brothers and sisters in Islam, we are the products of Allah (s.w.t.). Allah (s.w.t.) made each and every one of us. So how could we **say** or **think** or **feel** that the product of Allah (s.w.t.) is ugly? How could we think such a thing? How dare we! How dare we feel, think or believe that the creation of Allah (s.w.t.) is worthless? In other words my brothers and sisters, how could you feel bad about who you are?

I want to tell you something my dear readers about myself—a trait that made me hate myself. When I stretch out the palms of my hand, you can see that my palms are different. They are different in colour. As you are reading, you're probably thinking "Oh, I knew he was an alien or something." But that is just me. That is how my real hands are and there is a difference in colour. My students back in Australia, asked me "Brother, are your hands made out of plastic?" NO. These are my real hands. In fact, I used to tell my students back in Australia that I would give $10,000 to anyone who could bring me a man or a woman—not from my family—who has hands like mine.

Guess what?

You will never find it because this is unique to the Wael Ibrahim's family, from my mum's side *subḥānAllāh*. We don't even know what it is. Even the doctors don't know what it is and the cause of it. But it's there and I love them now. I am even giving lectures about my hand. *Allāhu Akbar*. This is the product of Allah (s.w.t.). So how could we look at them and say ugly? You are indirectly saying that Allah (s.w.t.) is not wise enough to make something perfect, *walā ʾaʿūdhubillāh*, or you are accusing the perfection of Allah (s.w.t.).

This is actually an area where you can fall into *shirk* and *kufr*, and we don't want to get into that. When you say "I am worthless," remember your self-worth. There are, of course, some people who do go through these experiences. These people deem themselves worthless and feel that they don't deserve goodness and that they are the worst. May Allah (s.w.t.) protect you. Thus, it is important to remember and know your self-worth. Just knowing that Allah is your Creator is sufficient for your self-worth. Allah (s.w.t.) says in the Qur'an:

۞ وَلَقَدْ كَرَّمْنَا بَنِيٓ ءَادَمَ ... ﴿٧٠﴾

And We have certainly honoured the children of Adam...

(Surah al-Isra', 17:70)

"Most certainly we have dignified and honoured the children of Adam." If Allah has dignified our status, then how could we look down upon ourselves? This is the self-love that will bring you closer and closer to Allah (s.w.t.).

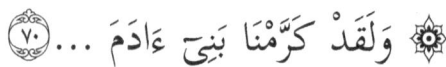

Chapter 3

Self-Love as a Way of Life

Let us dive into how we can exercise and practise self-love.

Loving Others

How to exercise self-love? First and foremost, you have to love others for the sake of Allah (s.w.t.). You have to love your fellow brothers and sisters for the sake of Allah (s.w.t.).

What does it actually mean to love your brother and sister for the sake of Allah? It means that I love you without expecting anything in return—nothing whatsoever. Let me give you an example. I invite you for a meal without expecting that you will invite me for a meal. Another instance is I give you a gift for the sake of Allah, purely for the sake of Allah without even thinking; that because you are rich, you are a politician or an actor, or anything, you will in return give me something more expensive.

Do you know those people who randomly call you sometimes and say "*Salam*. How are you? How is your mum? How is your dad? How's your brother? How's your uncle? How's your job?"—and of course you are replying to all their questions nicely by saying "Yes *alḥamdulillāh*. How are you?" and so on. After the long-winded questions from them about how your family is, the person will say "Hey, listen. I need you to do me a favour."

Focus with me here my dear readers. Is the person calling you to ask you about your family and their well-being or for the favour? It's the favour. Some people say that the long-winded question is ethics. People say that this is ethical. NO. These are not ethics. This is semi-hypocrisy. The person is calling and just making an introduction; by asking about the well-being of the other person and his family members. But the reality is the person who is calling does not care about the man or woman they have called. The only care about the favour.

How many of us have experienced this? I know some of us have.

The fact that we were a friend with someone for many years and when the moment we fall, the first one to disappear is them—the one who we thought was our best friend. And then suddenly, they randomly call out of the blue for a favour. True or false?

In a nutshell, the first tip to help you develop self-love is to love others.

Let us now get into an interesting activity. I want you to say something to your family, friends, co-workers, or the person beside you while you are reading this book (just make sure it's not the opposite gender unless you're in a halal relationship with them). I want you to say to them "I love you for the sake of Allah" and they too have to respond and say "May the one whom you love me for His sake love you also."

This is a beautiful activity. This is something that the companions used to practise in the life of the Prophet Muḥammad (s.a.w.). In fact, a man came to the Prophet (s.a.w.) and said to him "Can you see the man standing over there?" The Prophet (s.a.w.) said, "Yes." The man said, "I love him for the sake of Allah." The Prophet (s.a.w.) told the man to go and tell the person himself.

And so, if you love someone, go and tell them I love you for the sake of Allah (s.w.t) instead of just telling someone else and not doing anything. In return, the response should be "May the one whom you love me for His sake love you too.

Narrated Anas ibn Malik:

> A man was with the Prophet (s.a.w.) and a man passed by him and said: Messenger of Allah! I love this man. The Messenger of Allah (s.a.w.) then asked: Have you informed him? He replied: No. He said: Inform him. He then went to him and said: I love you for Allah's sake. He replied: May He for Whose sake you love me love you!
>
> (Sunan Abi Dawud 5125)

Editor's Note

This beautiful activity was conducted in the lecture hall by Shaykh Wael. All the participants told to the person beside them that they love each other for the sake of Allah. The hall was filled with smiles and laughter because of this heartwarming activity.

May Allah (s.w.t.) increase our love for one another. May Allah (s.w.t.) make this love a true and genuine one. May Allah (s.w.t.) make it a reason for us to be sheltered under the shade of Allah's throne—on the day where there would be no shade except Allah's shade. That is a promise. There are seven categories of people who will be sheltered under Allah's shade on the day of Judgement. One of the categories is two individuals who love each other for the sake of Allah (s.w.t.). These two individuals meet upon that love and they depart upon that love. They have no personal interest in one another—just genuine sincere love for the sake of Allah (s.w.t.).

Narrated Abu Hurayrah:

> The Prophet (s.a.w.) said, "Seven (people) will be shaded by Allah by His Shade on the Day of Resurrection when there will be no shade except His Shade. (They will be), a just ruler, a young man who has been brought up in the worship of Allah, a man who remembers Allah in seclusion and his eyes are then flooded with tears, a man whose heart is attached to mosques (offers his compulsory congregational prayers in the mosque), two men who love each other for Allah's Sake, a man who is called by a charming lady of noble birth to commit illegal sexual intercourse with her, and he says, 'I am afraid of Allah,' and (finally), a man who gives in charity so secretly that his left-hand does not know what his right hand has given."
>
> (Ṣaḥiḥ al-Bukhari 6806)

Honesty and Truthfulness

To some, this might sound silly but this is the truth. If you want to increase self-love in your life, you have to develop something cold. You have to develop honesty and truthfulness.

Do you agree that sometimes we actually lie to ourselves? I know you agree with me. Sometimes, we convince ourselves with something that we know is wrong. We know it is wrong and we lie about it. So, if you want to increase your self-worth, self-respect and values in your life—you then have to be honest and courageous enough to take responsibility for your actions. Moreover, when you err, be courageous enough to say "I'm sorry."

Do you agree with me that there are some cultures and communities in which sometimes in the hemisphere of marriage—the husband and wife have a relationship where it is very difficult for the husband to apologise to his wife? I know some of you are like "Yes, that's true" while reading this. However, some are vice versa also. So, no matter who it is, say sorry when you have erred. Sayyidina 'Umar al-Khaṭṭab (r.a.) once said:

> "Hold yourselves accountable before you are held accountable and evaluate yourselves before you are evaluated, for the Reckoning will be easier upon you tomorrow if you hold yourselves accountable today."
>
> (Muḥasabat al-Nafs 2)

Judge yourself my brothers and sisters in Islam. Judge yourself first before you are put to judgement by Allah (s.w.t.). Evaluate your life. Ask yourself,

Am I doing the right thing?

Is this something right?

Will this be accepted for me on the Day of Judgement?

Will I be among the people that the Prophet (s.a.w.) will give me a drink from his hands which will make me never feel thirsty again?

Or will the Prophet (s.a.w.) not look at me and tell me to go away?

Who do you want to be my dear readers? It is mentioned in the following hadith that some will not be given the water to quench their thirst on the Day of Judgement:

Abu Sa'id Al-Khudri added that the Prophet (s.a.w.) further said:

> "I will say those people are from me. It will be said, 'You do not know what changes and new things they did after you.' Then I will say, 'Far removed (from mercy), far removed (from mercy), those who changed (the religion) after me!"
>
> (Ṣaḥiḥ al-Bukhari 7051)

So, evaluate your life and your actions. What do you think are the actions that will *inshā'Allāh* result in our life being directed to *Jannah*? Think about it. In addition, be honest and tick the boxes. If you need to rectify any situation, or any mistake in your life, be brave and honest enough to rectify it.

Authentic

Be authentic.

Be yourself.

Don't worry about what people are going to say about you. For example, about your nose. "Oh this Shaykh has a big nose. Have you seen his nose? His nose is so big you know." Don't care about these kinds of comments. Don't worry about what people may think of you or what they might label you as. Don't allow anyone to define who you are. This is how Allah made you, so be authentic.

ʿAbdullah ibn Masʿud (r.a.) was describing to the other generation about the companions. He (r.a.) lived a little bit longer after the companions had passed away and he was talking about the companions to the other generation. He (r.a.) was telling them that whoever wanted to follow a path, a righteous path, should follow the path of those who passed away. Ibn Masʿud (r.a.) was referring to the companions of the Prophet (s.a.w.) because they died upon righteousness. Thus, when you follow them there will be no chance for us to be misguided if we follow them. They died.

If they were still alive, chances are there that they might be misled as the future is unknown. Basically, Ibn Masʿud (r.a.) is telling us that if you want to follow a path of righteousness, follow the righteous one's path, the path of those who have passed away: they are the companions of the Prophet (s.a.w.). Then he (r.a.) started listing down their qualities that the companions of the Prophet (s.a.w) were the best of this *ummah* and no one is better than the companions, no one is better than them after the prophets. And they have the most pious of all hearts—they have the most depth of the knowledge of the *din* of Allah (s.w.t.). The next thing he said is very important and I want you to focus with me here. He (r.a.) said that they were the least superficial. The companions were not trying to pretend to be someone else. They were very pure and authentic.

> "Whoever wants to follow an example, let him follow the example of those who have passed away, the Companions of Muḥammad (s.a.w). They were the best of this *ummah*, the purest in heart, the

> deepest in knowledge, the least in sophistication. They were people whom Allah chose to be the Companions of His Prophet (s.a.w.) and to convey His religion, so imitate their ways and behaviour, for they were following the Straight Path."

The companios were the **least** superficial—the least in sophistication. They were authentic. That is why for instance you will find stories of the man who came to the Prophet (s.a.w.) and said in front of the people "Ya Rasul allow me to commit adultery." Can you imagine this? What do you think will happen if you walk to a *masjid*, to the Imam and ask him "Imam, can you please make *zina* halal?" What will happen?

Mashā'Allāh Malaysian people are so kind and shy when I ask such questions. I was in an Asian country and *mashā'Allāh* I love these people so much, and that's why I pick and joke around with them all the time. So, I'm not shy to mention the country's name. It was in Pakistan and I threw this example as well. One of the brothers said that he would make the man into a minced beef. *Lā ḥawlā walā quwwata illā billāh.*

Back to the hadith, the man came to the Prophet (s.a.w.) and said to allow him to commit adultery. The Prophet (s.a.w.), in this narration, did not even say haram to the man even though it is haram. He (s.a.w.) did not mention the word haram but rather he reasoned with the man. The Prophet (s.a.w.) asked him if he was fine if something like this happened to his mother. The man said "NO. I want to do it but my mum NO, *astagfirullāh*." The Prophet (s.a.w.) continues to ask if it were acceptable for such a thing to happen to his wife, daughter, aunt and so on. The man replied "NO." Hence, the Prophet (s.a.w.) reasoned with him and explained to him that other people too do not want such a thing to happen to their mothers, daughters and so on. Then, the Prophet (s.a.w.) placed his hand on the man's heart and made *du'a'* for him. The Prophet (s.a.w.) made *du'a'* to remove the love of the haram from his heart.

> Abu 'Umamah reported: A young man came to the Prophet (s.a.w.), and he said, "O' Messenger of Allah, give me permission to commit adultery." The people turned to rebuke him, saying, "Quiet! Quiet!" The Prophet said, "Come here." The young man came close and he told him to sit down. The Prophet said, "Would

you like that for your mother?" The man said, "No, by Allah, may I be sacrificed for you." The Prophet said, "Neither would people like it for their mothers. Would you like that for your daughter?" The man said, "No, by Allah, may I be sacrificed for you." The Prophet said, "Neither would people like it for their daughters. Would you like that for your sister?" The man said, "No, by Allah, may I be sacrificed for you." The Prophet said, "Neither would people like it for their sisters. Would you like that for your aunts?" The man said, "No, by Allah, may I be sacrificed for you." The Prophet said, "Neither would people like it for their aunts." Then, the Prophet placed his hand on him and he said, "O' Allah, forgive his sins, purify his heart, and guard his chastity." After that, the young man never again inclined to anything sinful.

(Musnad Aḥmad 22211)

The point is people used to talk about their sins to get solutions and guidance from the Prophet (s.a.w.). And that, answers the question that always comes to me because I work in the area of addiction—undesirable activities like pornography and all that. Many people ask me, "But brother, isn't this exposing our sins?" You are coming to seek support and help. So how could this be punishable? If you are bragging about it, it is haram. If you are proud of it, it is haram. If you are showing off and telling people that you were watching this and that and so on, then of course, what you are doing is haram. You are actually exposing yourself when Allah has concealed it with His veil, whereby He has hidden your sin. Thus, if you announce and brag about your sins, then it is haram. The Prophet (s.a.w.) said in the hadith below:

"All the sins of my followers will be forgiven except those of the *Mujahirin* (those who commit a sin openly or disclose their sins to the people). An example of such disclosure is that a person commits a sin at night and though Allah screens it from the public, then he comes in the morning, and says, 'O' so-and-so, I did such-and-such (evil) deed yesterday,' though he spent his night screened by his Lord (none knowing about his sin) and in the morning he removes Allah's screen from himself."

(Ṣaḥiḥ al-Bukhari 6069)

The point is there is a difference between exposing your sins and talking about them privately, confidentially with a professional, with a Shaykh, or with someone who is trusted in the committee for one ultimate reason and that is to get rid of the sin. This is because some sins are considered addictive sins and you can't actually help yourself to get out of it alone. You do need someone else to support you. And so, one of them is for the addictive sins.

On a side note, addiction by definition is the rewiring of the brain function. So, the structure of your brain changes physically and as a result, you cannot control your own actions. So, you don't want to do the act, but you find yourself going into it over and over again, just like a rat in the lab. So how could you not ask for help? How will anyone be able to help you if they don't know what the sin is? Try to distinguish between these both my dear readers.

Confidence

Next, you must develop self-confidence. Every one of us is unique my dear brothers and sisters in Islam. Allah (s.w.t.) has gifted us with something that He did not give to someone else and you have to respect that. You don't need to compete with anyone.

Alḥamdulillāh, Allah has blessed me to be friends with so many Shaykhs. *Alḥamdulillāh.* You don't find me wearing exactly like this Shaykh or that Shaykh, or talking like a certain Shaykh; or talking about areas that other Shaykhs are an expert in. I had a different path. And so, I further developed in my path and *alḥamdulillāh,* I have become an expert in that path and area. What happens when you become an expert at something? You become confident to talk about it. Now, this can be applied in any facet of life; in your studies, work, messages and services. Some people, like my fellow Shaykhs and me, are standing on stage and delivering lectures and speeches as we have developed ourselves on this path. May Allah (s.w.t.) accept from all of us, *āmīn.*

On the other hand, my dear brothers and sisters, do you not think that you are also a part of the event that you join in? You are the participants. The money that you paid to make the event happen, don't you think that this is in the scale of your good deeds? That it could be considered actually as a charity that you have paid to bring *daʿwah* into your country; to bring the words of Allah (s.w.t.) into different parts of the world.

So, my job is to speak at lectures and events. The participant's job is to come and fill up the venue and then go out there and share the knowledge that they have learned. There are some brothers and sisters at the event, whose job is to just stand at the gates. They are not inside the hall to listen to the lectures. But do you think that they don't get the rewards? They do. They are just doing their job in that area to ensure the event goes smoothly. Thus, know your area and develop it. Develop it and become an expert and then be proud of it. Don't compare yourself with anyone.

Contentment

Be happy with who you are.

Be content with whatever Allah (s.w.t.) has given you.

What is *ar-riḍa*? It is contentment. Be content and happy with who you are. My brothers and sisters in Islam, it was said that ʿAli ibn Abi Ṭalib (r.a.) defined *taqwa*. What is *taqwa*? God-consciousness. For me, the word in the English language is very complicated because we don't use the word "God-consciousness" in regular conversation much. Do you say like "My consciousness is tired." NO. We don't talk like that. But God-consciousness means to develop self-awareness that Allah is watching you in public and private. As a result, you won't do nonsense. That is *taqwa*. You are not fearing Allah as an entity but you are feeling His punishment because you believe that Hellfire exists—that is *taqwa* in definition.

ʿAli ibn Abi Ṭalib (r.a.) added a few more points to the definition of *taqwa*. He (r.a.) said "to fear Allah and His punishment; to implement the knowledge and the revelation that Allah sent down from high which is the Qur'an and the teaching of the Prophet (s.a.w.); and to be content with whatever Allah has given you, **even if it is little**"—even if it is little from your perspective. This is because Allah (s.w.t.) always gives you what you **need**, not necessarily what you **want**.

What will happen if Allah (s.w.t.) gives us what we want all the time? We will destroy this earth. May Allah protect us all. The final point in the definition of *taqwa* by ʿAli ibn Abi Ṭalib (r.a.) is to prepare ourselves for the day of departure, death—the Day of Judgement. This is what we want to develop in ourselves *inshāʾAllāh*: to be content wherever we are *inshāʾAllāh*.

Tranquillity

The final point is *ṭuma'ninah* or tranquillity; to train yourself to be calm in the face of challenges.

My dear readers, three years ago, when I was washing my hands over the sink—as per the advice of the government during COVID—a severe crashing pain ran from my waist all the way to my legs; my toes and every inch of my lower back. In a split second, I was pinned to the ground and I could not move an inch for three hours. I was in that extremely uncomfortable position for three hours. My wife and my children ran to help me and get me up. However, every time they touched me, a shooting pain would snatch my nerves. The pain intensified as time went by. Later—may Allah bless my wife and children—they brought a blanket after three hours. They did not know how to get me out so they decided to put the blanket under me inch by inch. Afterwards, they dragged me out. Literally, they dragged me into my room. Now this took me to a two-to-three-month period of depression. Focus on this word, "depression." People will usually respond "You Shaykh Wael in depression? *Astagfirullāh.*" "You don't have *iman.*" "*Astagfirullāh.* I'm not gonna listen to you anymore."

We are humans—that's who we are. The pain I felt was intense. It was excruciating. However, *subḥānAllāh*, there was this one Shaykh who helped me get through the test. May Allah bless him. It is Shaykh Haitam al-Haddad from the United Kingdom. He gave me a call, and asked me "How are you, man?" And I cried. Immediately I started crying. I told him "I can't take it Shaykh." I kept complaining and complaining about my pain. He said to me "What's wrong with you?" I said, "I'm telling you Shaykh you don't feel what I feel." Shaykh Haitam said "I don't care whether I feel what you feel or not because that is not the point. Why are you complaining about your pain when instead you can focus on the reward?"

Look at this lesson closely my brothers and sisters because this is what woke me up instantly and at that moment, I decided to get back on my feet *alḥamdulillāh* by Allah's will. Shaykh Haitam said "This is not my concern. My concern is why don't you focus on the reward? The Prophet (s.a.w.) said that even a thorn that may poke you, will eliminate your sins. Now you are in a desperate situation of too much pain and so the reward would be tremendous only if you exercise patience. If you say to Allah that you accept what He has given you and you will go through it, I'm sure there will be wisdom out of it." *SubḥānAllāh.*

Narrated Abu Sa'id Al-Khudri and Abu Hurayrah:

> The Prophet (s.a.w.) said, "No fatigue, nor disease, nor sorrow, nor sadness, nor hurt, nor distress befalls a Muslim, even if it were the prick he receives from a thorn, but that Allah expiates some of his sins for that."
>
> (Ṣaḥiḥ al-Bukhari 5641)

SubḥānAllāh, later a book was produced and written by me to help people with their pain. *Allāhu Akbar.* Then, *ṭuma'ninah,* tranquillity.

I want to tell you about another Shaykh. He is Shaykh Abu Ishaq al-Heweny. He is a very popular Shaykh from Egypt who specialises in the sciences of hadith. One of his legs was amputated. And so, this one other Shaykh visited him in the hospital and told Shaykh Abu Ishaq, "Shaykh be patient. Allah is testing you." He replied, "You be patient. I'm good *alḥamdulillāh.*" Later on in an interview, someone asked Shaykh Abu Ishaq, "How does it feel that you are now in a wheelchair and people are pushing you around? How do you feel? Do you feel sad? Shaykh Abu Ishaq said "NO. I can see my leg flying, preceding me to *Jannah.* Why would I feel sad when a part of me is going to *Jannah* before me?" *SubḥānAllāh.* That is *ṭuma'ninah* and acceptance. So, try and achieve that state of tranquility my brothers and sisters.

Chapter 4

Conclusion

Before ending, I want you my dear brothers and sisters to do a little activity. I want you to look at someone. Look at them in the eye and say "I am awesome." Do it with them. Say it together "We are awesome." How does it feel when you do that? Why are we awesome? Because we are the creation of Allah (s.w.t.). What more awesomeness do you want in your life? *Allāhu Akbar.* That is why you say:

...وَإِنَّآ إِلَيْهِ رَٰجِعُونَ ﴿١٥٦﴾

...Indeed we belong to Allah, and indeed to Him we will return.

(Surah al-Baqarah, 2:156)

I spoke a bit about my story about my back and how I was paralysed for over a year in a wheelchair and so on in the previous chapter. Of course, those who have read my book, *My Wheelchair* would know more. The thing is before I end, I want to let you know about this *ayah* so you can use it for your journey in life—for your soul and yourself. The *ayah* above actually brought me back on my feet. *'Innā li-llāhi wa-'innā 'ilayhi rāji'ūn*—the *ayah* that we associate with **death**. However, this is the *ayah* that you should cling to whenever your life becomes dark. You know where you are going; you are going to Allah (s.w.t.). So why should you fear? Why should you be sad? Of course, when I mention this, I do not mean that you should delete the emotions. What I mean is to not let the sadness go to the point where it consumes you and swallows you as a whole.

So be sad if you want to be sad. We are humans. It is OK to be sad. There are no negative emotions anyway. I do not believe that emotions are negative. It is we who have made them so actually. We are the ones who have made emotions negative. We are the ones who tell people to not feel at all the emotion of sadness. A lot of the time, when you tell someone that you are sad, they will respond by telling you to not be sad. And then you switch off your feelings or you delete sadness from your life like an app. NO. That is not it. That is not the way. That is just what we have done. So, change it and remember that we are humans. If you feel sad as a result of a situation, so be it. Just make sure you are not sad for too long that you will fall into the void that will make your life harder; which will then make you go astray from Allah (s.w.t.).

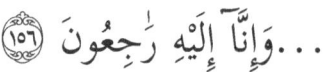

At the same time, remember to grow from what you have experienced. Practise self-love. Remind yourself that you have been honoured and that you are the creation of Allah (s.w.t.).

All that I have discussed, my dear brothers and sisters in Islam if we could put in practice bit by bit, one tip at a time—by not rushing anything—we will increase our self-worth on the side of Allah (s.w.t) before anyone else, *inshā'Allāh*. *Inshā'Allāh* that will make us respect ourselves and never look down upon anyone.

May Allah (s.w.t.) make us see through ourselves the ability to change the condition of the *ummah* for the better. *Amīn ya rabbal 'alamīn. JazakAllāh khayr*. I love you all for the sake of Allah (s.w.t.). *Assalamu 'alaikum warahmatullāhi wabarakatuh.*

Muhammad and Me

Mufti Ismail Menk

Table of Contents

Preface **51**

Introduction **53**

Chapter 1: The Prophet and me **62**
The Impact and Legacy of Prophet Muḥammad (s.a.w.) 63
The Extraordinary Selection of Messengers 65
Close Circle and Early Believers in the Message 68
The Test of Faith and Patience 70
Would You Have Accepted His Message? 72
Sending Salutations and Blessings upon Muḥammad (s.a.w.) 74
The Destructive Nature of Jealousy 76
If You Should Love Allah, Then Follow Me 78

Chapter 2: The Untarnished Reputation of the Miraculous One **80**
The Prophet's Reputation: Impervious to Harm 81

Chapter 3: *Raḥmatan lil-'Alamin* **86**
Allah's Divine Message: A Mercy to the Worlds 87
Mercy Toward Animals and Humanity 88
Forgiveness and Reconciliation: The Prophet's Approach 89
Handling Negativity and Criticism The Prophet's Way (s.a.w.) 92
Allah's Love for Those Who Do Good 93

Chapter 4: Beyond the Ordinary **95**
The Perfect Creation: The Prophet Muḥammad (s.a.w.) 96
The One Who Luminates Like the Moon 97
The Prophet's Life: A Pathway to Understanding Islam 99
Miracles and Blessings in Nature: Connecting with the Prophet 100

Chapter 5: Balancing Spirituality in Modern Comforts **103**
Prophet Muḥammad and Worldly Comforts 104
Reflecting on the Magnificence of Creation 108
The Last Person to Enter Paradise: A Reward Beyond Comprehension 109

Closing Thoughts and Prayer **110**

Preface

The life of Prophet Muḥammad (s.a.w.), shines through the radiant pages of history as a guiding light, illuminating the path for the believers. In the Qur'an, Allah Almighty extols his character to such a magnificent degree that he is positioned as the greatest model for humanity (Surah al-Qalam, 68:4). And once he was sent by Allah (s.w.t.), his life became an evidence of this assertion. Not only that, but the depth of his love that he has for the believers, both those who shared his life at the time and those who came after him, was unbounded by the passage of time.

As a messenger sent to us by Allah Almighty, he made it very clear to us that our salvation depends on following his example. The Prophet Muḥammad (s.a.w.) was quoted saying,

> "The likeness of me and the likeness of my nation is of a man who kindled a fire in which animals and moths started falling. You are plunging headlong into it while I am grabbing onto the knots of your lower garments to prevent you from falling therein."
>
> (Ṣaḥiḥ al-Bukhari 6483)

This analogy reflects his limitless love and care for the well-being of all people.

Nurturing this love requires us to go on a journey of reflection and comprehension—by totally immersing ourselves in the example set by our beloved Prophet (s.a.w.) both in his words and deeds. His life serves as a blueprint for honesty and integrity, exemplified by his pre-prophethood titles *as-Ṣadiq*—the Truthful and *al-Amin*—the Trustworthy.

In the countless layers of a materialistic world, following in his footsteps requires an unshakeable commitment. It encourages the believers to navigate the currents of material pursuits while simultaneously grounding themselves in the principles that the Prophet Muḥammad (s.a.w.) articulated and put into practice. In the face of difficulties, maintaining a firm commitment to his values turns into a guiding light for resilience and a demonstration of our commitment to a more meaningful life.

This section of the book will take you on a journey through aspects of the life of the Prophet Muḥammad (s.a.w.). May it inspire you to incorporate his teachings into the very fabric of your life, and may it deepen your love for him (s.a.w.).

Mufti Menk

Introduction

Assalamu ʿalaikum warahmatullāhi wabarakatuh. It is truly a pleasure to be here in Malaysia after several years, reflecting on the challenges brought about by the pandemic, which, *SubḥānAllāh*, distanced us to some extent. However, despite these physical separations, we may have connected online during this time. We express gratitude to Allah for granting us the privilege of being here today, sharing this moment for His sake.

When we gather, it is important to ensure our meetings hold meaning and purpose. This significance can manifest in various ways, whether related to worldly matters such as health or wealth, or, most importantly, in discussing the profound issues set by Allah (s.w.t.). So, let us thank Allah and congratulate ourselves for contributing to the success of this event. Without your support, it would not have been possible

Consider that when you purchased a ticket or offered your financial support, you became a vital contributor to this noble cause. You played a role in making this event possible, and, in essence, you were a mini-sponsor. This principle extends to daily activities, just as when you contribute to your local mosque's upkeep or operations. Even a modest contribution adds up to ensure that you bear the responsibility of maintaining the House of Allah and supporting your own use of its facilities.

In fact, each time you enter the mosque and benefit from its services, you should consider making a small donation, as this ensures that you are personally investing in the maintenance of this sacred place. Doing so not only fulfils your religious duty but also empowers you to contribute towards the mosque's expenses, making you accountable for your own usage.

If you were to donate a small sum for each prayer, how much would you give? It is difficult to put a specific value on it, right? However, if I were to suggest a contribution of RM1 or $1.00 for each prayer, every time you enter the mosque, it would sum up. Did you not benefit from the facility, the utilities, the lighting, the carpets, and everything else that was maintained for you? Others ensured the place was clean and well-kept. Therefore, you should consider contributing, even if it is just RM5 or your spare change. You can occasionally forgo a cup of *teh tarik* to support this cause. By doing so, you will have contributed not only to the upkeep of the House of Allah but also covered your own usage expenses, ensuring that you don't burden others. What's the point of fulfilling your religious duty, such as prayer, when others have covered all the costs, from electricity to facilities? Occasionally, contribute to the donation box, even if it is just a small amount.

Let us remember that all we discuss here is derived from the teachings of the Prophet Muḥammad (s.a.w.) and the guidance of Allah. Whether it is helping a charitable organisation in Africa or giving *zakat* to support those in need, our actions are rooted in the noble teachings of our faith, and they carry immense significance.

Have you ever thought about the process? You click "send", enter your card details, and your money is on its way. But have you considered what happens next? Let me remind you of my approach to this matter.

Someone will carry that money and deliver it to its intended destination, where it will meet those in need. And who does this delivery on your behalf? Not you, indeed. So, if you are making this contribution for your sake, there is an associated cost with transferring those funds from here to there. This cost is not borne by just one person or organisation; it is divided among many because charities often collect from thousands of donors and then distribute the aid.

In light of this, wouldn't it be more meaningful to add a few extra dollars or ringgits to your donation to help cover these costs? It is a more responsible way to ensure that your obligation under the pillar of Islam is fulfilled without burdening others. After all, there are expenses incurred in delivering your charity.

I recall an organisation that invited the less fortunate individuals to a central location, promising food hampers. However, when these individuals arrived, they had to pay for transportation from their villages to the designated place. Who should cover these transport costs? It is an issue that needs consideration. Why should someone in need be expected to pay for your *zakat* obligation to be fulfilled? You should be the one to provide for their transportation, even if it is just a few extra ringgits or one more dollar. This small addition can make a significant difference.

It is important to understand that, by recognising and assisting the less fortunate, you are fulfilling a great favour from Allah (s.w.t.). Consider yourself fortunate to have the means to help. A time may come when you are no longer able to do so.

Today, we're going to delve into a discussion about the *Prophet Muḥammad (s.a.w.) and Me.* "Me" in this context refers to you and me, to ourselves and our relationship with this incredible and beautiful creation of Allah. But who is the Prophet Muḥammad (s.a.w.)? It is essential to understand who he is.

Allah's knowledge is beyond our comprehension. He (s.w.t.) has already decreed everything, even before creating the universe. Allah's knowledge is so profound that it encompasses not only what will happen, but also what will never happen and what could have happened if it did. When you reflect on your life and consider the choices that you have made, know that Allah already knows how it would have altered your life.

There are times when we desperately want something, but Allah does not grant it because He knows it is not in our best interest. So, pray to Allah and say, "O' Allah, if it is good for me, grant it to me. If it is not, then keep it away." If you don't receive what you asked for, believe in your heart that, despite your intense desires and cries for it, it was not meant for you. Move forward because life is short, with the longest life span barely reaching 100 years. Even 100 years might seem short in the eyes of Allah. It is just a small fragment in the grand scheme of time, which is a creation of Allah. His knowledge is boundless and profound.

يعلم ما كان وما يكون وما لم يكن لو كان كيف سيكون

He knows what was, what will be, and what was not, and if it had been, what it would be like.

Indeed, Allah's knowledge is awe-inspiring. He encompasses the past, present, and future, and even that which will never come to pass—how it would be if it were to be. This depth of knowledge is truly remarkable.

Allah (s.w.t.), in His infinite wisdom, created the Prophet Muḥammad (s.a.w.), just as He created Adam (a.s.) from a blend of dust and water, forming a shape from the elements of the Earth, and then breathed a soul into him, bringing him to life. What's fascinating is that Adam (a.s.) was created as an adult, and he possessed unique qualities. He was already able to speak and had knowledge of the names of all things from the very moment of his creation. This creation was unlike any other, demonstrating the extraordinary power and wisdom of Allah.

وَعَلَّمَ ءَادَمَ ٱلْأَسْمَآءَ كُلَّهَا ثُمَّ عَرَضَهُمْ عَلَى ٱلْمَلَٰٓئِكَةِ
فَقَالَ أَنۢبِـُٔونِى بِأَسْمَآءِ هَٰٓؤُلَآءِ إِن كُنتُمْ صَٰدِقِينَ ﴿٣١﴾

And He taught Adam the names—all of them. Then He showed them to the angels and said, "Inform Me of the names of these, if you are truthful."

(Surah al-Baqarah, 2:31)

This is a verse from Surah al-Baqarah and it is indeed a beautiful and significant verse. It emphasises that Allah taught Adam (a.s.) the names of all things, and Adam (a.s.) already knew them when he was created. He could identify objects like trees, the sky, mountains, water, and more.

As for the language that Adam (a.s.) spoke, it is not explicitly mentioned in the Qur'an, and we do not have detailed information about it. Some people speculate that it could have been Arabic, but the truth is—we do not have definitive evidence to confirm the language. It is worth noting that languages have evolved over time, and the concept of specific languages like English or Malay as we know them today might not exist during the time of Adam (a.s.).

And so, the exact language Adam (a.s.) spoke remains unknown, and it is not crucial to our faith or understanding of Islam. What's important is the message and guidance from Allah, regardless of the language through which it was conveyed. It is all in the realm of Allah's knowledge, and speculation about the specific language is not a central concern in Islamic teachings. It is always interesting to contemplate, but we must remember that these details are not the primary focus of the Qur'an's message. The Qur'an's guidance transcends linguistic specifics and addresses matters of faith, morality, and human conduct.

Certainly, it is a valid perspective to consider that the existence of the Prophet Muḥammad (s.a.w.) in some form was already planned by Allah—especially if we reflect on the broader context of Islamic belief. According to Islamic tradition, Allah created Adam (a.s.) and Eve (Hawwa') as the first human beings, and all of humanity is believed to be their descendants. The Prophet Muḥammad (s.a.w.) is also a part of this human lineage.

In this sense, it could be viewed that the existence of the Prophet Muḥammad (s.a.w.) was part of Allah's divine plan from the very beginning when He created the first human beings, Adam (a.s.) and Hawwa'(r.a.). This belief reflects the concept of prophethood in Islam, where Allah selects certain individuals to convey His guidance and message to humanity at different times and places.

So, your observation aligns with the idea that the Prophet Muḥammad's role in delivering Allah's message to humanity was predetermined as part of the broader plan of creation and guidance.

Allah (s.w.t.) says:

وَإِذْ أَخَذَ رَبُّكَ مِنۢ بَنِىٓ ءَادَمَ مِن ظُهُورِهِمْ ذُرِّيَّتَهُمْ
وَأَشْهَدَهُمْ عَلَىٰٓ أَنفُسِهِمْ أَلَسْتُ بِرَبِّكُمْ ۖ قَالُوا۟
بَلَىٰ ۛ شَهِدْنَآ ۛ أَن تَقُولُوا۟ يَوْمَ ٱلْقِيَـٰمَةِ إِنَّا كُنَّا عَنْ
هَـٰذَا غَـٰفِلِينَ ﴿١٧٢﴾

And [mention] when your Lord took from the children of Adam—from their loins—their descendants and made them testify of themselves, [saying to them], "Am I not your Lord?" They said, "Yes, we have testified." [This]—lest you should say on the Day of Resurrection, "Indeed, we were of this unaware."

(Surah al-A'raf, 7:172)

Allah mentions that He extracted or removed from the back of Adam (a.s.) all the souls that were destined to come into existence, encompassing all of humanity, extending from that moment until the end of time. In a pre-eternal gathering, Allah posed a question to these souls, asking, "Am I not your Lord?" To this, every soul bore witness and affirmed, "Indeed, you are our Lord." Allah admonishes humanity not to forget this covenant and to remember this day of acknowledgement.

This concept relates to the *fiṭrah*, which can be understood as the primordial and uncontaminated nature of human beings. The *fiṭrah* signifies the inherent inclination and recognition of the oneness of Allah that is instilled in every human soul. It is a profound reminder of our spiritual connection with our Creator and the fundamental principles of monotheism. That word, **uncontaminated**, is absolutely important because the hadith says:

> Allah's Messenger (s.a.w.) said, "Every child is born with a true faith of Islam (i.e. to worship none but Allah Alone) but his parents convert him to Judaism, Christianity or Magainism, as an animal delivers a perfect baby animal..."
>
> (Ṣaḥiḥ al-Bukhari 1359)

It is essential to recognise that no individual is inherently born with a particular religious or spiritual disposition, except that they are innately endowed with *fiṭrah*. This concept is elucidated in the words of Allah Almighty, where it is unequivocally stated that parents play a pivotal role in either preserving this *fiṭrah* or potentially influencing their offspring's beliefs and perspectives in a certain direction. A hadith underscores this idea, emphasising that parents have the capacity to mould their children into adherents of various faiths—including Judaism, Christianity, or Islam. This underscores the fact that, if uncontaminated, individuals possess an innate capacity to discern right from wrong independently.

However, as one matures and is exposed to their environment, their perception becomes subject to external influences, akin to how a smartphone's factory settings evolve as one downloads applications. Initially, when you acquire a new phone, it contains only a few pre-installed functions and ample storage space. Similarly, as one grows older and encounters various experiences, their belief system and moral compass are shaped by the environment they inhabit.

It is worth contemplating how one's perception of "normal" is invariably influenced by the surroundings they are exposed to. For instance, the advent of mobile phones was once inconceivable, but today, young children are not only aware of their existence but also proficient in using them—including unlocking devices with facial recognition. This demonstrates how familiarity with technology becomes a norm within a particular generation due to their upbringing and environment.

In light of this, it is vital to revisit the *fiṭrah* that Allah created humanity upon. At the inception of human existence, Allah posed the question to all souls, "Am I not your Lord?" to which they responded in affirmation. This fundamental recognition is imprinted in human nature, guiding individuals toward acknowledging a Supreme Deity and Creator who fashioned everything, including humanity and the prophets, most notably Prophet Muḥammad (s.a.w.).

Allah Almighty has meticulously designed humanity, with the DNA of Adam (a.s.) serving as the common thread that runs through generations. Conducting a DNA test would likely reveal a familial connection between any two individuals, extending back approximately 15 to 30 generations or more. It is conceivable that humanity shares a common forefather, with distant ancestral ties binding us together.

Moreover, as technology and research advance, it is plausible that we will uncover more evidence that refutes the theory of human evolution from apes. The theory of evolution is multifaceted and lacks a singular perspective, making it a broad and nuanced topic. However, as science progresses, it may substantiate the belief that humans did not evolve from apes, aligning with the divine narrative.

One day, a man seated beside me initiated a conversation. He proceeded to inquire about the theory of evolution, prompting me with the question, "What are your thoughts on the theory of evolution?" In response, I found myself somewhat speechless, as the topic is undeniably vast and encompasses numerous facets.

I replied, "Well, it is such a complex subject with multifaceted aspects. What specifically are you referring to?" He clarified, "Evolution, the idea that humans evolved from apes." To this, I quipped, "Perhaps you descended from apes, but I am a product of humanity."

It is also essential to acknowledge certain references to historical incidents where people were transformed into apes, as mentioned in sacred texts. These references should be approached with an understanding of their metaphorical or symbolic significance, rather than taken literally.

قُلْ هَلْ أُنَبِّئُكُم بِشَرٍّ مِّن ذَٰلِكَ مَثُوبَةً عِندَ ٱللَّهِ ۚ مَن لَّعَنَهُ ٱللَّهُ وَغَضِبَ عَلَيْهِ وَجَعَلَ مِنْهُمُ ٱلْقِرَدَةَ وَٱلْخَنَازِيرَ وَعَبَدَ ٱلطَّٰغُوتَ ۚ أُو۟لَٰٓئِكَ شَرٌّ مَّكَانًا وَأَضَلُّ عَن سَوَآءِ ٱلسَّبِيلِ ﴿٦٠﴾

Say, "Shall I inform you of [what is] worse than that as penalty from Allah? [it is that of] those whom Allah has cursed and with whom He became angry and made of them apes and pigs and slaves of *ṭāghūt*. Those are worse in position and further astray from the sound way"

(Surah al-Ma'idah, 5:60)

In Islam, it is emphasised that all human beings are equal in the sight of Allah, regardless of their lineage or background. Our status and worth are determined by our faith and good deeds, not our ancestral origins.

As for the Prophet Muḥammad (s.a.w.), he is indeed regarded as the final messenger, the seal of the prophets, and the most noble of all of them. As Muslims, we believe that he was created in a most perfect and beautiful manner; "خلقت مبرأ من كل عيب" (created free from all defects).

While every prophet in Islam is honoured and respected, the Prophet Muḥammad (s.a.w.) holds a unique and unparalleled position due to his role as the final messenger and the one who completed and perfected the message of monotheism and guidance for humanity.

Allah (s.w.t.) says:

۞ تِلْكَ ٱلرُّسُلُ فَضَّلْنَا بَعْضَهُمْ عَلَىٰ بَعْضٍ ۘ مِّنْهُم مَّن
كَلَّمَ ٱللَّهُ ۖ وَرَفَعَ بَعْضَهُمْ دَرَجَٰتٍ ۚ ... ﴿٢٥٣﴾

Those messengers—some of them We caused to exceed others. Among them were those to whom Allah spoke, and He raised some of them in degree…

(Surah al-Baqarah, 2:253)

Chapter 1

The Prophet and me

The Impact and Legacy of Prophet Muḥammad (s.a.w.)

Your connection with the Prophet Muḥammad (s.a.w.) is rooted in your belief in his prophethood and the recognition of his extraordinary status as the final and most comprehensive messenger of Allah. In Islamic belief, he is indeed regarded as the greatest of creation, the most noble of all prophets, and the seal of the Prophets.

The Prophet Muḥammad (s.a.w.) holds a unique place in history and religion. He is not only the first to enter *Jannah* but he also has the largest number of followers among all the prophets. This is a testament to the profound impact of his message and his role in guiding the majority of humanity to the worship of the one true God, Allah.

Prophet Muḥammad (s.a.w.) speaks about the massive number of his followers on the Day of Judgement, reflecting his unique and central position in the prophetic tradition. This hadith emphasises the immense influence and significance of his message throughout human history.

As a believer, your connection with the Prophet Muḥammad (s.a.w.) is through your faith, your love for him, and your dedication to following his teachings and examples. His life and message continue to inspire and guide Muslims worldwide. It is truly remarkable to remember and consider that the Prophet Muḥammad (s.a.w.) lived in a time without technology, without any means of communication like we have today—let alone social media platforms like Facebook, Instagram, Twitter or TikTok. Yet, his message has reached and influenced billions of people throughout history. The exponential growth of the Muslim *ummah* is a testament to the timeless and universal nature of the message he conveyed.

The fact that the Prophet (s.a.w.) was informed by Allah that he would have the greatest and largest *ummah* is a reflection of the divine knowledge and wisdom. This was a part of Allah's plan, and it is one of the signs of the prophethood of Muḥammad (s.a.w.).

Today, indeed, the Muslim *ummah* is vast and diverse, with more than 2 billion people around the world who bear witness that Muḥammad is the Messenger of Allah. His legacy, his teachings, and his example continue to resonate and guide the lives of countless individuals, serving as a source of inspiration, guidance, and unity for Muslims globally. The enduring impact of the Prophet Muḥammad's (s.a.w.) message is a testament to the strength and universality of his mission.

I recall a particular day when I assisted someone in their journey to Islam. I tend to inquire whenever I have the opportunity: "What inspired your conversion to Islam?" The gentleman, who happened to be an elderly individual, shared his thoughts. He said, "I've observed people and various religions for an extensive period. Let me tell you something profound: the multitude of pilgrims I've witnessed coming in and out of Makkah on television cannot all be mistaken simultaneously. It is inconceivable. Moreover, their message is astounding. They call people back to their innate disposition, the natural inclination to worship the one true Lord. When one is in touch with their true nature, certain truths become evident. Among them is the recognition of a divine Creator—the source of our existence."

He continued, "Some argue that humans emerged by mere chance, a random occurrence in the vastness of nature. But, if it was indeed a coincidence, why did it occur only once? Why hasn't it happened again? Can you explain that? I'm waiting for a second 'pop', but it never happened. I say this with respect to their beliefs; we're not here to harbour hatred. We're merely expressing our faith."

"Allah, the Almighty, states that if one's nature remains pure, they'll recognise the need to worship their Creator. It is a natural instinct. Whoever brought us into existence deserves our worship, and we shall worship Him alone. That's it. So, who is the Creator, you might ask? Whoever He is, we refer to Him as Allah, the Worshipped One, the sole deity deserving of our worship, the Supreme Being. When I declare '*Allāhu Akbar*,' I'm proclaiming that the One who fashioned me is the Greatest. This statement is irrefutable."

The Extraordinary Selection of Messengers

Who is the Greatest? The One who created us holds that title. Following Him, the greatest is the one He designates. For us, it is the Prophet Muḥammad (s.a.w.), and subsequently, there are four others, each chosen and designated by Allah as elite messengers. We accept them as the top-tier messengers of God.

ٱللَّهُ يَصْطَفِى مِنَ ٱلْمَلَٰٓئِكَةِ رُسُلًا وَمِنَ ٱلنَّاسِ ۚ إِنَّ ٱللَّهَ سَمِيعٌۢ بَصِيرٌ ﴿٧٥﴾

> Allah chooses from the angels messengers and from the people. Indeed, Allah is Hearing and Seeing.
>
> (Surah al-Ḥajj, 22:75)

Allah's selection of messengers is a meticulous process. He carefully chooses individuals from both the angelic realm and among humanity. You might recognise some angelic names. For instance, the foremost among all angels is Jibra'il. Can you name another angel? Mikail. Another one? Israfil. How about another? 'Izra'il. Now, humorously, you might find it interesting that my father named me Ismail. Speaking of Ismail, I have a friend in South Africa named Ismail, and we often chuckle about this connection. He told me once, "You know what my father says? He thinks you're an angel." I asked, "Why?" He humorously replied, "Because of the '*eel*' at the end of your name, *Māshā'Allāh*." It is all in good fun, but, as with any name, there are both virtuous and less virtuous individuals who carry it, and we ask for Allah's forgiveness.

Allah (s.w.t.) selects His messengers from among the angels, choosing those whom He deems appropriate to bear His divine message. This selection is entirely within His prerogative, and His choices are absolute. Similarly, among human beings, Allah designates certain individuals for this sacred task. In this context, Allah identifies a distinguished group of messengers known as *Ulul 'Azm*. These are individuals who demonstrated exceptional dedication, made significant efforts, and left an indelible mark in their mission.

The Qur'an is replete with accounts of these exceptional messengers, with narratives detailing the lives and trials of individuals such as Musa (a.s.) and Ibrahim (a.s.), who offered immense sacrifices and laid the foundation for prophethood. Ibrahim is acknowledged as *Abul-Anbiya'* or the "father of the prophets" for the significant role he played in shaping the prophetic lineage, with his descendants including Ismail and Ishaq, who were also recipients of prophethood.

The five most distinguished messengers in this select group are as follows:

1. Muḥammad (s.a.w.)
2. Nuh (Noah, a.s.)
3. Ibrahim (Abraham, a.s.)
4. Musa (Moses, a.s.)
5. Isa (Jesus, a.s.)

These five occupy a unique and exceptional circle within the prophetic tradition, each making a profound impact on the course of human history.

وَإِذْ أَخَذْنَا مِنَ ٱلنَّبِيِّـۧنَ مِيثَـٰقَهُمْ وَمِنكَ وَمِن نُّوحٍ
وَإِبْرَٰهِيمَ وَمُوسَىٰ وَعِيسَى ٱبْنِ مَرْيَمَ ۖ وَأَخَذْنَا مِنْهُم
مِّيثَـٰقًا غَلِيظًا ٧

> And [mention, O' Muḥammad], when We took from the prophets their covenant and from you and from Noah and Abraham and Moses and Jesus, the son of Mary; and We took from them a solemn covenant
>
> (Surah al-Aḥzab, 33:7)

Allah Almighty specifically mentions these distinguished names in Surah al-Aḥzab, often referring to them together, emphasising their collective significance as the *Ulul 'Azm* or those of great determination. These five prophets have demonstrated remarkable dedication and resolute commitment in fulfilling their divine missions. This is not to diminish the determination of other prophets; rather, it highlights the exceptional role and challenges faced by these five.

When Allah chooses a person for a specific task or mission, it is an absolute divine selection, and no one can object or have a say in the matter. The Prophet Muḥammad (s.a.w.) faced ridicule, mockery, and opposition when he received the divine message in Makkah. However, his close friends and inner circle were the first to believe in him. They reasoned that since he had never lied to them in worldly matters, he could be trusted in matters of the hereafter, especially when his message was to worship the One who created them—a message that bore no personal gain for him but was solely for the benefit of humanity.

يا أيها الناس، قولوا لا إله إلا الله تفلحوا

O' people say there is none worthy of worship besides Allah and you will be successful

(Musnad Aḥmad 23192)

Indeed, the central message of the Prophet Muḥammad (s.a.w.) during his time in Makkah was the simple and profound declaration: "يا أيها الناس، قولوا لا إله إلا الله تفلحوا" (O' people, say, 'There is no deity but Allah,' and you will be successful). His mission was to call people to the worship of the one true God, Allah, and to affirm monotheism. He consistently emphasised that he was a messenger of Allah, not a deity to be worshipped or revered in the same way. His message was clear: worship the Creator, not the creation.

قُلْ يَٰٓأَيُّهَا ٱلنَّاسُ إِنَّمَآ أَنَا۠ لَكُمْ نَذِيرٌ مُّبِينٌ ﴿٤٩﴾

Say, "O' people, I am only to you a clear warner."

(Surah al-Ḥajj, 22:49)

Close Circle and Early Believers in the Message

The support of one's closest circle, especially family and those who know us intimately, is a powerful testament to one's character and trustworthiness. In the case of the Prophet Muḥammad (s.a.w.), his closest friends and, notably, his wife Khadijah (r.a.) were the first to believe in his message. Their unwavering belief and trust in him were rooted in their deep knowledge of his character and conduct.

Khadijah (r.a.) displayed extraordinary faith and trust in her husband. After descending from the hill where the Prophet had sought solitude, deep in meditation, Angel Jibra'il (a.s.) appeared with the first words of revelation, "*Iqra'*." You are familiar with these initial words, aren't you? "Read." Anyway, after this profound encounter, he returned and confided in his wife, saying, "*Zammiluni*," or "Envelope me," which, in our terms, could be akin to asking for a warm, loving embrace. It is remarkable how he approached his wife in such a tender manner. In contemporary times, some spouses might ask, "Why?" "What's the story behind this sudden request for a hug?"

When he recounted his experience, Khadijah (r.a.) responded with an emphatic, "*Kalla, wallāhi*," which is one of my favourite expressions from Khadijah (r.a.). In fact, it is one of my favourite things she has ever said. She looked at her husband and declared, "No, by Allah, I solemnly swear he will never forsake you because you are a righteous man." *Allāhu Akbar*! The unwavering support of a spouse is truly remarkable. She assured him, "Don't worry. You won't be let down. We will find out what this means. Let's consult my cousin, Waraqah. He's knowledgeable; he'll guide us." It is quite remarkable to see how she proactively took the initiative to say to her husband, "Come, let's visit Waraqah and see what he has to say."

Waraqah bin Nawfal (r.a.) conveyed, "You know, that was indeed the Angel who came to you. The day he instructs you to proclaim, I will support your message if I'm alive." Khadijah bint Khuwaylid (r.a.) affirmed, "You are a person who fulfils the rights of everyone, going out of your way to be kind and compassionate. Allah (s.w.t.) will not let you down."

Khadijah's unwavering support and her ability to see the goodness in her husband set a beautiful example of trust and mutual respect in a marital relationship. Her confidence in his character was a crucial source of encouragement and validation during the early days of his prophethood. It serves as a timeless example of the importance of a supportive and trusting family and spouse, especially during significant life challenges and transitions.

Additionally, the acceptance of the Prophet Muḥammad's (s.a.w.) message by his closest circle, including his dear friend Abu Bakr (r.a.), carries a profound lesson about trust and integrity.

When the Prophet Muḥammad (s.a.w.) embarked on his mission, he delivered a simple yet powerful message: to worship the One who created them. His closest friends, including Abu Bakr, were the first to embrace this message. Their acceptance demonstrated their complete trust in the Prophet—recognising his honesty, trustworthiness, and the consistency of his character.

This episode offers an essential piece of advice for everyone in the modern context as well, especially with the advent of social media. In today's world, we often interact with people we may not personally know, and they may pass judgements, comments, or criticisms based on limited information or misperceptions. It is crucial to remember that negative comments or judgements from individuals who do not truly know you should not define your self-worth.

The Prophet Muḥammad (s.a.w.) emphasised the importance of being the best to your family and spouse. This inner circle, composed of those who live with you and know you intimately, holds a special place. Their testimony and understanding of your character are invaluable. It is within these close relationships that your true character and values are most clearly revealed. Therefore, being good and trustworthy to those who truly know you, and to those who stand as witnesses to your character is of utmost significance. Their recognition and endorsement speak volumes about your integrity and worth.

The Test of Faith and Patience

My brothers and sisters, when you go out of your way to be kind and respectful to anyone and everyone that you come across, Allah will never let you down. Evidence of it is what Khadijah (r.a.) said. If something negative is happening in your life today, it can never be negative for a true believer.

Abu Yaḥya Ṣuhaib bin Sinan (r.a.) reported that:

> The Messenger of Allah (s.a.w.) said, "How wonderful is the case of a believer; there is good for him in everything and this applies only to a believer. If prosperity attends him, he expresses gratitude to Allah and that is good for him; and if adversity befalls him, he endures it patiently and that is better for him". [Muslim]
>
> (Riyaḍ aṣ-Ṣaliḥin 27)

The affairs of the believers are amazing. Nothing negative can ever happen to them. No matter what happens, it is always goodness actually that will happen to a believer. Let me give you an example. Let's say something negative came in your direction. You bore *ṣabr* when that trial happened. *Ṣabr* is an act of worship that nobody can engage in except the one whom Allah has tested. It is said in the Qur'an:

...إِنَّ ٱللَّهَ مَعَ ٱلصَّٰبِرِينَ ١٥٣

...Allah is with the patient.

(Surah al-Baqarah, 2:153)

Indeed, *ṣabr* is a virtue highly regarded in Islam, and it comes in various forms. It encompasses enduring hardships, staying steadfast in fulfilling your religious obligations and abstaining from sinful actions. Patience is not limited to simply bearing difficulties; it also includes exercising self-control and perseverance in all aspects of life.

Allah (s.w.t.) promises His presence and support to those who exercise patience. When we face tests, trials, and challenges, whether in fulfilling our religious duties or in refraining from sinful behaviours, we demonstrate our faith and commitment to Allah. In these moments, we turn to Allah for strength and guidance—relying on Him to help us remain steadfast.

Every act of patience is an act of worship, and it brings us closer to Allah (s.w.t.). Patience helps us maintain our faith and protect ourselves from wrongdoing. It is a powerful tool for personal growth and spiritual development.

Take a moment to reflect on this: how do those closest to you perceive your character? Are they witnesses to your goodness? If not, it is never too late to make a positive change. Starting today, strive to be a better person. Be truthful, upright, and helpful. Avoid causing unnecessary hardships, especially for your family and loved ones. Remember, when you make life difficult for someone, it creates a debt, and that debt will be repaid—whether in this world or the Hereafter. On the Day of Judgement, there will be no escape, and every secret will be laid bare. Let us pray for Allah's forgiveness for our shortcomings.

Prophet Muḥammad (s.a.w.), and the unwavering support he received, was a remarkable testament to his prophethood. His wife, Khadijah (r.a.), believed in him from the very beginning. Many of us, including myself, sometimes struggle to gain the trust and belief of our spouses. You say something, and they might respond with scepticism—regardless of what you believe or think. It is a common human experience.

Yet, consider the beautiful example of the wife of Prophet Muḥammad (s.a.w.). His wife, Khadijah (r.a.), was the first to believe in him without hesitation. She did not question him when he shared his extraordinary experiences, such as the visitation by the Angel. Can you imagine telling someone that an Angel appeared to you, and their immediate response is, "Did that really happen?" No, we don't usually see this level of trust. Thus, it is truly remarkable that she believed in him wholeheartedly.

Furthermore, when the Prophet (s.a.w.) and Khadijah (r.a.) recounted these experiences to their close circle, 'Ali (r.a.), who lived with them, immediately believed him as well. He was a young boy at the time. Among the adult males, Abu Bakr Ṣiddiq (r.a.) was the first to believe. Among the adult females, it was Khadijah (r.a.). These were the initial three, the closest supporters. Following them, the Prophet's friends and those who had interacted with him over time gradually recognised his role as a messenger.

May Allah grant us the honour of being resurrected as the friends of the Prophet Muḥammad (s.a.w.) on the Day of Judgement. *Āmīn.*

Would You Have Accepted His Message?

I want you to ponder upon this my dear brothers and sisters. If you were present during the time of the Prophet (s.a.w.), would you have accepted his message? It is a thought-provoking question, isn't it? Now, let's fast forward to today. The distinction between what is halal and haram is clear, and the do's and don'ts in Islam are well-established. The teachings of the Prophet (s.a.w.) are accessible to us. However, many of us who claim to be followers of Islam still don't fully accept his message.

Consider this: when the companions of the Prophet (s.a.w.) learned that alcohol and intoxicants were prohibited, they immediately discarded them. Contrast that with our behaviour today. When we are aware that certain things are forbidden, we often hesitate to abandon them or worse—we persist in sinful actions.

Let us pray that Allah grants us the strength to do what is right. Let us prioritise our five daily prayers, a fundamental pillar of Islam. *Fajr*, *Dhuhr*, *'Asr*, *Maghrib*, and *'Isha'* are the five daily prayers. Some of us, however, tend to prioritise *Dhuhr*, *'Asr*, *Maghrib*, and *'Isha'*, while *Fajr* becomes a missed opportunity. We know the saying, "If you snooze, you lose," and in this case, it is more than just a saying—it is a reality.

So whenever you disobey an instruction of Allah given by Rasulullah (s.a.w.), tell yourself: "I need to strengthen myself. If I'm a true follower, I have to get up for *Ṣalatul Fajr*." Furthermore, the Prophet Muḥammad (s.a.w.) tells us that the two units of prayer prior to the *farḍ* of *Fajr* are better than the whole world and whatever it has. It is mentioned in the following hadith:

رَكْعَتَا الْفَجْرِ خَيْرٌ مِنَ الدُّنْيَا وَمَا فِيهَا

The two *rak'ah* at dawn are better than this world and what it contains.

(Ṣaḥiḥ Muslim 725a)

This is exactly how it is worded in the hadith. The hadith says the two units of prayer prior to the *farḍ*, which means the sunnah of *Fajr* is better than the whole world and whatever it has. I want to ask you a question: if that is better than the whole world and whatever it has—then what do you think is the value of the *taḥajjud*?

تَتَجَافَىٰ جُنُوبُهُمْ عَنِ ٱلْمَضَاجِعِ يَدْعُونَ رَبَّهُمْ خَوْفًا وَطَمَعًا وَمِمَّا رَزَقْنَٰهُمْ يُنفِقُونَ ﴿١٦﴾

> Their sides part [i.e., they arise] from [their] beds; they supplicate their Lord in fear and aspiration, and from what We have provided them, they spend.
>
> (Surah as-Sajdah, 32:16)

In Surah as-Sajdah, Allah (s.w.t.) describes a special group of people who draw close to Him. These individuals forsake their comfortable bedding at night, standing in prayer with a blend of hope and fear in their hearts. They hope for Allah's mercy while fearing His wrath and punishment. Ṭhey engage in *taḥajjud*—the late-night prayer, and it is essential to recognise the significance of this act.

Taḥajjud is by invitation only—it is extended only to those whom He chooses. When you engage in *taḥajjud*, you are essentially accepting this divine invitation. It is Allah who empowers you to rise at that moment, putting the inclination in your heart to get up, perform ablution, and pray. The very act of *taḥajjud* is a blessing from Allah, granted to you by His grace.

If you are among those who perform *taḥajjud*, you deserve to be congratulated for embracing this spiritual practice. However, it is vital to remember not to let it inflate your ego or create a sense of superiority. The moment you develop such an attitude, *shayṭan* has successfully tainted your good deeds. In reality, we are all part of the same journey and struggle in our quest to come closer to Allah. We should always maintain humility and gratitude for any acts of worship we are blessed to perform.

Sending Salutations and Blessings upon Muḥammad (s.a.w.)

What is the significance of extending our supplications and greetings to the Prophet Muḥammad (s.a.w.)? It is essential to grasp the profound importance of this practice. When Allah (s.w.t.) selects an individual for His divine favour—recognising and honouring that favour is tantamount to acknowledging Allah Himself.

When the Prophet Muḥammad (s.a.w.) was chosen by Allah, he was appointed as a prophet and a messenger, while the rest of us were chosen as followers. We were not selected to become prophets or messengers, but we were **indeed** chosen to be followers of Nabi Muḥammad (s.a.w.). Each time we hear his name, it is an opportunity for us to express our gratitude for the favour that Allah has bestowed upon us. We should be grateful for being followers of the greatest creation of Allah. We should thank Allah for accepting us and enabling us to worship Him alone while following his outstanding messenger.

اللَّهُمَّ صَلِّ عَلَى مُحَمَّدٍ، وَعَلَى آلِ مُحَمَّدٍ، كَمَا صَلَّيْتَ عَلَى إِبْرَاهِيمَ وَعَلَى آلِ إِبْرَاهِيمَ، إِنَّكَ حَمِيدٌ مَجِيدٌ، اللَّهُمَّ بَارِكْ عَلَى مُحَمَّدٍ، وَعَلَى آلِ مُحَمَّدٍ، كَمَا بَارَكْتَ عَلَى إِبْرَاهِيمَ، وَعَلَى آلِ إِبْرَاهِيمَ، إِنَّكَ حَمِيدٌ مَجِيدٌ

O' Allah! Send Your Mercy on Muḥammad and on the family of Muḥammad, as You sent Your Mercy on Abraham and on the family of Abraham, for You are the Most Praise-worthy, the Most Glorious. O' Allah! Send Your Blessings on Muḥammad and the family of Muḥammad, as You sent your Blessings on Abraham and on the family of Abraham, for You are the Most Praise-worthy, the Most Glorious.

(Ṣaḥiḥ al-Bukhari 3307)

The Destructive Nature of Jealousy

إياكـم والحسـد، فإن الحسـد يأكل الحسـنات كمـا تأكل النـار الحطـب

Beware of envy because envy consumes (destroys) the virtues just as the fire consumes the firewood

(Riyaḍ aṣ-Ṣaliḥin 1569)

This is a statement of the Prophet (s.a.w.). Jealousy corrodes your good deeds in a manner akin to how fire devours a dry log. Why does jealousy erode your good deeds? Let us consider a worldly example. Imagine someone attaining great wealth through lawful means suddenly—we are not discussing illicit gains in this example. This individual becomes a millionaire, and people typically react in different ways.

First, some may remain unaware of this person's newfound wealth. Others respond positively, saying, "*Māshā'Allāh*, you've done remarkably well. May Allah bless you, and may He grant me similar success." This response reflects genuine happiness and a heartfelt prayer for success.

However, a distinct category of people may speculate negatively—suggesting that the millionaire must be involved in illicit activities, tax evasion, or some form of dishonesty to accumulate such wealth. They might even insinuate that the person is using their legitimate business as a front. Such cynicism is unwarranted unless backed by concrete evidence.

It is essential to respond positively and sincerely by saying, "*Alḥamdulillāh*, *Māshā'Allāh*, *TabārakAllāh*. May Allah bestow more blessings upon them." Instead of harbouring negative thoughts, it is more rewarding to express happiness for others when Allah blesses them. After all, it is Allah who initially granted them these favours. Avoiding jealousy is a way to worship Allah, acknowledge His bounties, and preserve the purity of your heart.

The message that the Prophet Muḥammad (s.a.w.) brought is filled with goodness and guidance. He reaffirmed the fundamental principles, including what is often referred to as the Ten Commandments. In addition to reinforcing these principles, the Prophet Muḥammad (s.a.w.) introduced a comprehensive set of teachings that guide every aspect of our lives. These teachings are designed to liberate us in the truest sense.

For example, when the Prophet instructed us regarding our dress code, it was to liberate us from the shackles of societal expectations and the opinions of others. By adhering to his guidance on modesty and dress, we free ourselves from the pressures of external appearances. We dress for ourselves and for the sake of Allah—rather than for the judgements of others. This is true liberation.

Furthermore, the Prophet's teachings extend to financial transactions as well. By conducting our financial dealings in accordance with the principles of Islamic finance, we achieve true liberation. We live on Earth, but we must always remember that our life here is temporary, while our life in the hereafter is eternal. All the rules and regulations provided by the Prophet Muḥammad (s.a.w.) are an honour for us to fulfil. He taught us to live upright and honest lives, obtaining our needs through legitimate means and channels. If we cannot do so, we should abstain from those actions. Following this guidance allows us to prepare for our eternal life while living in accordance with the values and principles of Islam. May Allah grant us ease in doing so.

Indeed, every time we hear the name of Muḥammad (s.a.w.), we should send blessings and salutations upon him. There is no need to feel ashamed; in fact, it is encouraged. The Prophet Muḥammad (s.a.w.) taught us that when we send blessings and salutations upon him, Allah blesses us tenfold in return. Therefore, we should say, "May Allah bless him (s.a.w.)" with a sincere heart and without any feelings of jealousy. Our intention is to ask Allah to bestow even more blessings upon the Prophet (s.a.w.) who is already greatly blessed. Jealousy should have no place in our hearts.

If You Should Love Allah, Then Follow Me

Place in our hearts this belief dear brother and sisters:

Indeed, I am a follower of the Prophet Muḥammad (s.a.w.), who is the greatest and final messenger of Allah.

The Prophet's statement, "I am the last of the messengers. There is no messenger to come after me," is a clear testament to this fact. As a messenger, he brought the message **from** Allah, which is the Qur'an. It is important to acknowledge that the message is from Allah and not from the Prophet himself. Throughout the Qur'an, the Prophet Muḥammad (s.a.w.) never claimed to be the Lord or asked for worship. His message was to invite people to worship Allah alone and to follow his guidance. Following the messenger means following his teachings and the message he delivered, which is the Qur'an. This is a fundamental aspect of our faith.

قُلْ إِن كُنتُمْ تُحِبُّونَ ٱللَّهَ فَٱتَّبِعُونِى يُحْبِبْكُمُ ٱللَّهُ وَيَغْفِرْ
لَكُمْ ذُنُوبَكُمْ ۗ وَٱللَّهُ غَفُورٌ رَّحِيمٌ ﴿٣١﴾

Say, [O' Muḥammad], "If you should love Allah, then follow me, [so] Allah will love you and forgive you your sins. And Allah is Forgiving and Merciful."

(Surah Ali-ʿImran, 3:31)

"If you truly love Allah, then follow me," the Prophet Muḥammad (s.a.w.) emphasised. He did not say, "Worship me," but rather, "Follow me." By doing so, Allah will love you and forgive your sins. So, strive to follow his example to the best of your ability. Every aspect of the Prophet's life has been meticulously recorded: his actions, expressions, demeanour, appearance, and more. Whether he smiled or frowned, how he walked, the intricacies of his appearance, his size, the way he sat, drank, ate, dressed, and interacted with his wives—every detail is meticulously documented. It is a truly remarkable testament to his life. Nabi Muḥammad (s.a.w.) is the only person in existence whose entire life on Earth has been meticulously recorded—from A to Z, spanning from the beginning to the end. There is no other human being's life you can know in great detail except the Prophet's as everything is thoroughly recorded. Isn't this an extraordinary honour?

During the Prophet Muḥammad's (s.a.w.) time, those who opposed him sought excuses to undermine and divert people's attention away from him. What were some of the actions that they took? Let me highlight some of these critical points. These actions illustrate the contrast between the believers' relationship with the Prophet Muḥammad (s.a.w.) and the stance of those who disbelieved.

At that time, the leaders of Makkah openly declared their disbelief because they feared that if they accepted what the Prophet (s.a.w.) conveyed, he would become the leader, and they would lose their positions of leadership. This fear of losing their authority and status motivated their opposition. For example, one of these leaders, Abu Jahal (also known as ʿAmr ibn Hisham), actively opposed the Prophet (s.a.w.) because he was concerned about losing his leadership position.

What did they do to undermine the Prophet? They seized upon any perceived flaws, although in reality, there was little to criticise. They magnified insignificant issues. For instance, they baselessly accused the Prophet of being a madman. *Astaghfirullāh.* In regards to the false accusation, Allah (s.w.t) mentions a rebuttal in the Qur'an:

وَمَا صَاحِبُكُم بِمَجْنُونٍ ﴿٢٢﴾

And your companion [i.e., Prophet Muḥammad (s.a.w.)] is not [at all] mad.

(Surah at-Takwir, 81:22)

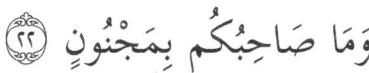

Chapter 2

The Untarnished Reputation of the Miraculous One

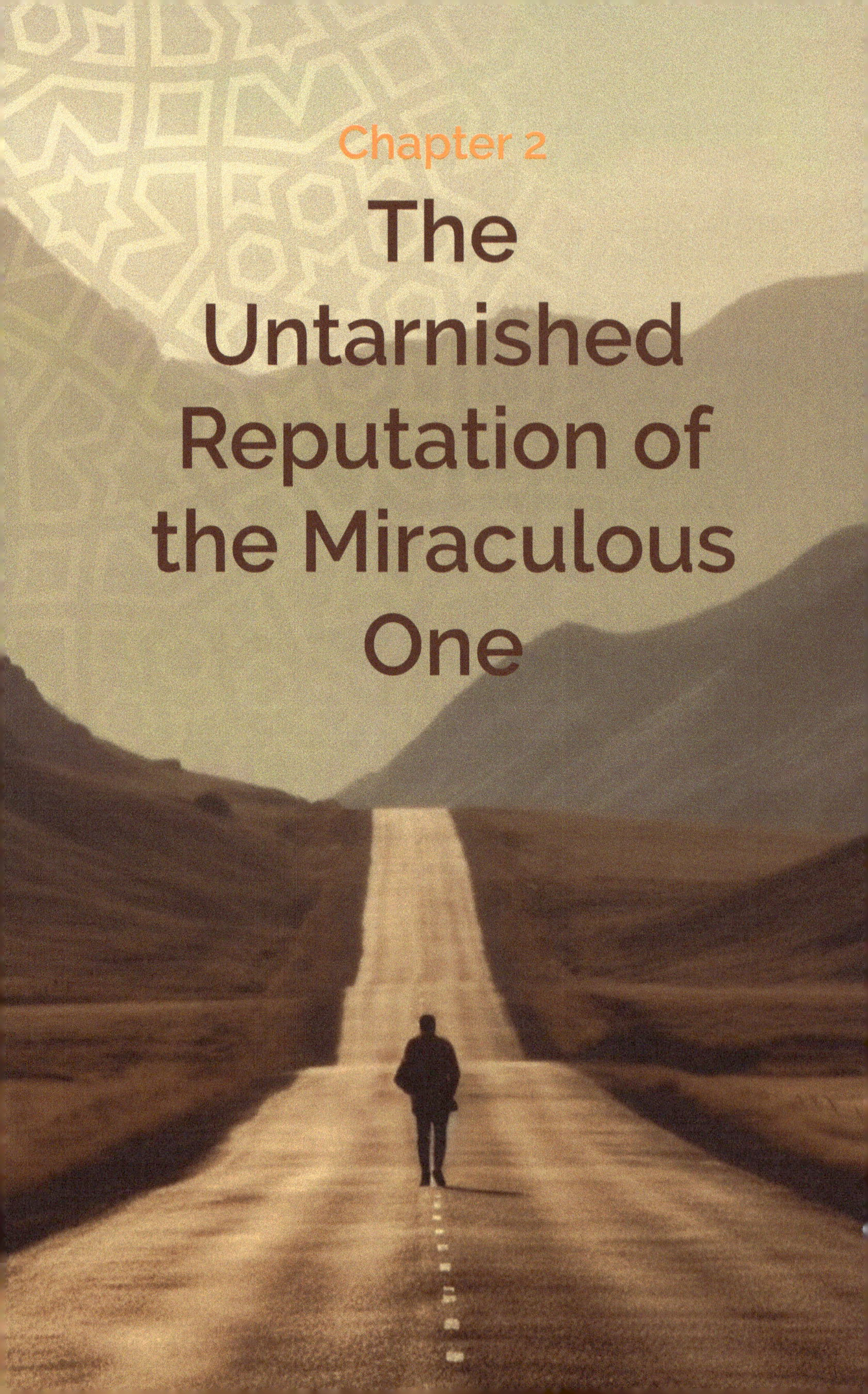

The Prophet's Reputation: Impervious to Harm

When the enemies of Prophet Muḥammad (s.a.w.) sought to discredit him, they resorted to various baseless accusations. They called him a womaniser. However, time proved them entirely wrong. The Prophet had only one wife at a certain point—which was Khadijah (r.a.). She was older than the Prophet (s.a.w.) and she was the mother of his children. Some narrations suggest she was much older, potentially 40 years old when he was 25, while others propose she was 28 when he was 25. The discrepancy in narrations is because, at that time, people did not consistently document people's age; they gauged the individuals' age through observation.

In addition, it is important to note as well that his enemies at the time never raised concerns about his marriage to ʿA'ishah—in regards to her age and the union itself. The entire community, including his fiercest adversaries, accepted it without dispute. However, 1400 years later, some individuals chose to raise issues about it despite the historical relevance and acceptance of the matter during the Prophet's time. We live in a different timeline than the Prophet (s.a.w.) so some things back in the day were different. And so in regards to the mockery against the Prophet (s.a.w.), Allah (s.w.t.) says in the Qur'an:

إِنَّا كَفَيْنَٰكَ ٱلْمُسْتَهْزِءِينَ ﴿٩٥﴾

Indeed, We are sufficient for you against the mockers.

(Surah al-Ḥijr, 15:95)

The reputation of the Prophet Muḥammad (s.a.w.) remains unblemished and impervious to harm. Those who laugh, scoff, mock, or jeer at him cannot diminish his exalted status. I assure you dear brother and sisters that every time someone has sought to blaspheme our beloved Prophet, more and more people have embraced Islam as a direct consequence of such blasphemy. This is a testament to the divine blessing that emanates from these attempts to malign him.

Even when individuals have burned the Qur'an, their actions have unwittingly spurred thousands of people to study the Qur'an, ultimately leading many to embrace Islam. This is a remarkable way in which Allah introduces His guidance to the world. It underscores the fact that the status and honour of the Prophet Muḥammad (s.w.t.) requires our defence—though we defend out of reverence and honour. Allah, the Almighty, safeguards his status and honour, irrespective of our efforts.

Allah (s.w.t.) says:

...وَٱللَّهُ يَعْصِمُكَ مِنَ ٱلنَّاسِ ۗ ...﴿٦٧﴾

...And Allah will protect you from the people...

(Surah al-Ma'idah, 5:67)

In the Qur'an, Allah has revealed verses affirming His divine protection for His chosen messengers—which includes safeguarding them from harm both physically and in terms of their reputation. Prophet Muḥammad (s.a.w.) experienced this divine protection in various ways, and his physical safety was assured.

A remarkable example of this protection can be seen in the case of Khalid ibn Walid ibn Mughirah (r.a.), a renowned warrior who initially opposed the Muslims. Upon his conversion to Islam, he shared an enlightening testimony with those around him. He recounted his experiences in battles where he and others had relentlessly attempted to harm the Muslims. However, he expressed that there was one individual whom they could never inflict any harm upon no matter how hard they tried. It was as if this individual was enveloped in divine protection. Khalid declared that this person was none other than our beloved Prophet Muḥammad (s.a.w.), demonstrating the miraculous safeguarding of the Prophet both physically and spiritually.

Indeed, the Prophet Muḥammad (s.a.w.) is the greatest of all, and no one can harm him. His enemies could not harm him physically, and they will never be able to tarnish his reputation. Even nowadays, some people create videos, cartoons, and other forms of slander against the Prophet (s.a.w.). However, this has often backfired them. Some of these individuals who attempted to defame him eventually embraced Islam as they realised the beauty of the Prophet's character and message.

Additionally, some of those who tried to destroy his reputation ended up damaging their own standing. Many of them suffered from mental health challenges, with some requiring medication for psychological disorders. It is essential to recognise that they are often victims of misinformation, which fuels their hatred toward the Prophet Muḥammad (s.a.w.).

From the days of Prophet Muḥammad (s.a.w.), consider the challenging episode in *Ṭāʾif* when people sought to harm him. Despite the adversity, his message and character continued to radiate, drawing numerous hearts towards Islam. The Angels had offered to crush the people of *Ṭāʾif*, the Prophet Muḥammad (s.a.w.) says:

Narrated ʿAbdullah:

> As if I saw the Prophet (s.a.w.) talking about one of the prophets whose nation had beaten him and caused him to bleed, while he was cleaning the blood off his face and saying, "O' Allah! Forgive my nation, for they have no knowledge."
>
> (Ṣaḥiḥ al-Bukhari 3477)

The Prophet (s.a.w.) knew that many people have been victims of misinformation and ignorance. They did not know the true character and mission of the Prophet Muḥammad (s.a.w.). Over time, as they learned more, many of them embraced Islam.

In addition, the enemies of the Prophet (s.a.w.) accused him of pursuing women, wealth, power, and position, but these claims were baseless. He was married to Khadijah (r.a.) during the peak of his life. At that time, he was 25 years old, and she was a widow in her 40s. She was his only wife for many years, and their union was characterised by deep love and respect.

Later on, the Prophet (s.a.w.) married widows and divorced women for noble purposes—to support and protect them. Each of these marriages had a specific reason and was never driven by base desires.

No matter what accusations were hurled against him, they backfired on those who made them. The truth of his character and the beauty of his message continue to shine and attract people to Islam. It is essential for individuals to seek accurate information from credible sources to understand the life and mission of the Prophet Muḥammad (s.a.w.).

During the victory of Makkah, Abu Sufyan ibn Ḥarb, one of the leaders of Quraysh, made a significant decision. He came forward to declare his *shahadah* and acknowledge the truth of Islam. He admitted that the reason they had initially denied the message of the Prophet Muḥammad (s.a.w.) was not because they believed he was lying but because they were concerned about how embracing Islam would alter the demographics of society. Their resistance was based on fear of change.

Many people hesitate to accept the truth because they anticipate that it will bring significant changes to their lives, which can be initially uncomfortable. For example, someone who wishes to don the hijab or dress modestly may worry about how their family and peers will react. They may anticipate resistance and pressure to conform to the status quo. However, when you choose to be steadfast in your beliefs and follow the path of righteousness, you are seeking the acceptance of Allah. This commitment may come with challenges, difficulties, and hardship, but it is a sign of your dedication to the truth.

I want to share a story of a non-Muslim woman online who practises black magic and casts spells for people. It is important to know that as believers, we are strictly prohibited from casting spells. The Prophet Muḥammad (s.a.w.) said that whoever casts a spell has associated partners with Allah and engaged in the gravest of sins. The same applies to those who seek the services of spellcasters.

Many people nowadays turn to practitioners of magic and witchcraft, like *bomoh*. These individuals claim to solve problems through magic, but the first thing they affect is your faith. By seeking their services, you risk losing your faith and need to renew your *shahadah*. This is a serious matter that should not be taken lightly.

The Messenger of Allah (s.a.w.) said:

> ...or who goes to a fortuneteller and believes what he says, he has disbelieved in that which was revealed to Muḥammad.
>
> (Sunan ibn Majah 639)

Back to the "magic lady", it is quite remarkable how this lady, who practises magic, openly admitted that there are instances when she cannot cast spells on people, and she attributed this inability to Muslims who pray five times a day. She described it as if there is a protective dome around such individuals known as "agrego." This is a non-Muslim's testimony about the strength and protection derived from faith and consistent prayer. It is a powerful affirmation of the spiritual fortitude that stems from acts of worship.

Talking about protection, one can't help but think of *Ayatul Kursi* and the last few surahs of the Qur'an known as the *mu'awwidhatayn*—which Muslims are encouraged to recite in the morning and evening for protection. This testimony underscores the efficacy of these practices in safeguarding believers from harmful influences and negative forces.

In addition to the issue of magic, there is another significant problem in society, which is the accusation of innocent people of witchcraft. This is a serious matter that can lead to false accusations and the breaking of relationships with innocent individuals. It is crucial to avoid baseless accusations and to always rely on proper evidence.

As believers, we should strive to uphold the principles of justice, fairness, and the protection of innocent individuals. May Allah Almighty guide and protect us all.

Chapter 3

Raḥmatan lil-'Alamin

Allah's Divine Message: A Mercy to the Worlds

It is indeed fascinating to contemplate the immense favour and blessing that Allah granted to humanity by sending the Prophet Muḥammad (s.a.w.) as a mercy to all the worlds.

وَمَآ أَرْسَلْنَٰكَ إِلَّا رَحْمَةً لِّلْعَٰلَمِينَ ﴿١٠٧﴾

And We have not sent you, [O' Muḥammad], except as a mercy to the worlds.

(Surah al-Anbiya', 21:107)

Allah (s.w.t.) has clearly stated in the Qur'an that He sent the Prophet Muḥammad (s.a.w.) as a mercy not only to mankind but to all of creation. He sent the Prophet as a messenger, teacher and guide for all. He sent the Prophet to teach us how to be merciful to not only human beings but also to animals and all other living beings.

And so, when Allah has chosen us to be a part of the *ummah* of the Prophet Muḥammad (s.a.w.), it signifies a tremendous honour. By Allah's will, His mercy, and the intercession of the Prophet Muḥammad (s.a.w.), we hope to enter Paradise.

The Prophet (s.a.w.) has conveyed the comforting message that he will recognise his followers on the Day of Judgement by the radiant marks on the places they used to wash during *wuḍu'* so many times a day. He will acknowledge his *ummah* and intercede with Allah on their behalf. This intercession is a source of great hope for those who have committed sins, as the Prophet (s.a.w.) will advocate for the forgiveness of Allah for those who genuinely tried and continued to seek His forgiveness.

Indeed, the hope and the assurance of the Prophet's intercession are a source of immense solace and motivation for the believers. We should strive to maintain our faith and seek forgiveness continuously, relying on the boundless mercy and grace of Allah.

Mercy Toward Animals and Humanity

When Allah teaches us to be merciful even towards animals, it underscores the importance of compassion in our behaviour. If we are guided to show kindness to a dog, it emphasises how we should treat other human beings as well—especially in times of war. The teachings of Islam emphasise the importance of treating prisoners of war with dignity and respect. This includes not harming the elderly, disabled, women, and refraining from targeting places of worship. Even in the context of war, these are off-limits. Today, the treatment of prisoners in many parts of the world falls far short of these standards.

The Prophet Muḥammad (s.a.w.) provided a perfect example of how prisoners of war should be treated. He emphasised fairness, respect, providing them with food, clothing, and dignity. Many prisoners, upon experiencing such humane treatment, were drawn to Islam.

The Prophet's teachings also emphasised the respect and dignity of women. He said that the best of people are those who treat their women with the utmost kindness.

Abu Hurayrah narrated that The Messenger of Allah said:

> "The most complete of the believers in faith, is the one with the best character among them. And the best of you are those who are best to your women."
>
> (Jamiʿ at-Tirmidhi 1162)

This teaching is unique to Islam and serves as a reminder of the high status and importance of women within the faith.

In essence, the Prophet Muḥammad (s.a.w.) sets a profound example of mercy, compassion, and respect for all, leaving us with invaluable lessons and guidance for our own lives.

Forgiveness and Reconciliation: The Prophet's Approach

The conquest of Makkah, known as the *Fatḥu Makkah* or the victory of Makkah, was a significant event in the life of the Prophet Muḥammad (s.a.w.) and the early Muslim community. This event took place when the Muslim army, numbering tens of thousands, marched to Makkah. Many of these Muslims were previously forced to leave their homes in Makkah, known as *al-Muḥajirun*, and they had made the *ḥijrah* to Madinah. Years later, they returned to their homeland. However, as the Muslims entered Makkah, those who had previously opposed them, fought against them, and committed various atrocities against them were anxiously waiting. They knew that they were now at the mercy of the Muslims they had wronged. Some may have feared that retribution was imminent.

In this context, the Prophet Muḥammad (s.a.w.) addressed the people of Quraysh, the tribe of Makkah, and posed a question: "O' people of Quraysh, what do you think I'm going to do to you today?" His question carried a mix of anticipation, hope, and fear. The people of Quraysh could only imagine what might be in store for them. They all might think: "*We're probably all going to be executed here today.*"

The Prophet's approach in this critical moment serves as a profound lesson in leadership, forgiveness, and reconciliation. His conduct was a reflection of the magnanimity and mercy he displayed throughout his life. He approached this momentous occasion with wisdom and a desire for reconciliation—similar to the way Prophet Yusuf (a.s.) dealt with his brothers when they were ultimately exposed.

This event marked a turning point in the history of Makkah and demonstrated the mercy, compassion, and forgiveness that the Prophet Muḥammad (s.a.w.) extended even to those who had previously wronged him and his followers. He (s.a.w.) said to his enemies:

"You can go, for all of you are free and forgiven. There will be no retribution today."

The Prophet Muḥammad (s.a.w.) stands as a unique example in the history of mankind, particularly as a leader and a military commander. His approach to the victory of Makkah, marked by forgiveness, mercy, and reconciliation is unparalleled.

In the moment of triumph, when he had the entire city of Makkah at his mercy, he chose not to seek retribution or revenge but instead extend forgiveness and embrace reconciliation. This benevolent and compassionate approach was a reflection of his true mission as a mercy to all of humanity. It was a living example of the principles of justice and goodness that he sought to spread.

The Prophet's actions went against the conventional practices of military leaders throughout history, who often sought to eradicate their enemies. His emphasis was not on harming, killing, or eradicating, but on promoting justice and goodness. His leadership was a shining example of mercy and compassion even in moments of victory.

This unique example of the Prophet Muḥammad (s.a.w.) continues to inspire people worldwide, serving as a model for leaders, followers, and anyone seeking to build bridges, promote peace, and uphold the values of justice, forgiveness, and reconciliation. It highlights the essence of Islamic teachings that emphasise mercy and compassion, even in the face of adversity and victory.

The contrast between the forgiveness and reconciliation demonstrated by the Prophet Muḥammad (s.a.w.) and the conflicts and grudges that persist within families today is a thought-provoking reflection.

The Prophet Muḥammad (s.a.w.) exemplified the highest standard of forgiveness and compassion, even to his enemies. He declared, "Go, you are free," to the people of Quraysh, who had previously wronged and persecuted him and the Muslim community. In contrast, many families often struggle to extend the same forgiveness and reconciliation even to their brothers and sisters whom they share the same parents with.

Family conflicts, disputes, and grudges can persist for years, causing immense pain and division. The Prophet's example reminds us of the importance of resolving family issues and letting go of grudges. It is an opportunity to find peace, healing, and unity within the family. Islam encourages resolving disputes, upholding justice, and treating family members with kindness and respect.

Forgiveness and reconciliation do not mean giving up your rights or ignoring injustice. It means finding a way to address the issues and move forward without harbouring resentment. The heart is a vessel that reflects its contents. Filling it with goodness will radiate goodness in your interactions. Striving for justice is important, but it can be pursued with politeness, kindness, and a willingness to let go of grudges.

The reward for those who forgive for the sake of Allah and make amends with family members is significant. Such actions are highly valued in Islam, and on the Day of Judgement, there is a special reward for those who choose forgiveness, reconciliation, and the path of kindness. So, it is a call for us to follow the Prophet's example and strive for harmony and unity within our families while upholding justice and not holding grudges in our hearts.

Handling Negativity and Criticism The Prophet's Way (s.a.w.)

Relating to our connection to the Prophet Muḥammad (s.a.w.)—*Muḥammad and Me*—his teachings have had a profound impact on the way people deal with negativity and criticism, especially in the age of social media.

Nowadays, people often encounter negative comments, false accusations, and out-of-context quotes being used against them. It is easy for individuals to become targets of online attacks and criticism, and sometimes these attacks can be extreme and hurtful.

One of the remarkable lessons from the Prophet Muḥammad (s.a.w.) is the ability to forgive and show patience in the face of negativity. Instead of harbouring resentment or responding with more negativity, he exemplified the concept of "forgive and forget." He was often the target of insults and accusations, yet he forgave those who wronged him and responded with kindness.

This is a valuable lesson for individuals who might face similar challenges on social media today. By forgiving and not letting negativity affect their inner peace, they can maintain their focus on their relationship with Allah, their own character development, and the ultimate goal of attaining paradise. Negativity and criticism from others should not be a source of distress, but rather an opportunity for personal growth and patience. Remember this important equation:

Allah (s.w.t.) + the Messenger (s.a.w.) + I
= a spot in *Jannah*

This way, one can free themselves from the emotional burden of negativity and continue their journey towards spiritual growth and closeness to Allah. Holding onto grudges and resentment only harms one's own well-being and spiritual progress. Thus, the choice to forgive and let go is an empowering one.

Allah's Love for Those Who Do Good

...إِنَّ ٱللَّهَ يُحِبُّ ٱلْمُحْسِنِينَ ﴿١٩٥﴾

...indeed Allah loves the doers of good

(Surah al-Baqarah, 2:195)

...وَٱللَّهُ يُحِبُّ ٱلْمُحْسِنِينَ ﴿١٣٤﴾

...and Allah loves the doers of good

(Surah Ali-ʿImran, 3:134)

Allah (s.w.t.) loves those who do good, and one profound explanation of this concept is that when we do good to someone, it should not be solely based on whether we think they deserve it. Instead, we should do good because we firmly believe that Allah loves those who perform acts of kindness.

In essence, this places Allah at the centre of our actions. When we extend goodness to others, it becomes a matter between us and Allah, and the person on the receiving end is just the medium. Therefore, we must be good to people regardless of whether we think they deserve it or not, because we know Allah loves those who perform acts of kindness.

This approach empowers us to make people feel valued and important; not because we deem them worthy, but because we seek Allah's love. This is a reflection of the Prophet Muḥammad's (s.a.w.) teachings of how he treated people. His example encourages us to perform acts of goodness with sincerity—knowing that it is Allah's love we are striving for, rather than approval from others.

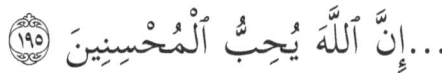

One of the most powerful aspects of the Prophet Muḥammad (s.a.w.) was that none of those around him ever felt that there was another person closer to him than themselves. He treated everyone with an abundance of love and importance. He would inquire about people's well-being, engage with them, and make them feel cherished and valued. When he interacted with someone, they felt that they were the most beloved to him.

This unique quality of the Prophet allowed everyone who encountered him to believe that they held a special place in his heart. He made each individual feel truly important. This was a miraculous aspect of his character. Despite having thousands of followers, everyone felt that they were the most beloved to him. This is a testament to the remarkable depth of his compassion and love. This is who our beloved Nabi (s.a.w.) is.

Chapter 4

Beyond the Ordinary

The Perfect Creation: The Prophet Muḥammad (s.a.w.)

The Prophet Muḥammad (s.a.w.) is known as the best of creation and the most noble of all prophets—the highest in every single way, created perfectly. In fact, Hassan ibn Thabit (r.a.), also known as the Poet of the Prophet (s.a.w.) said:

كأنك قد خلقت كما تشاء

As if you were created as you wish

The Prophet Muḥammad (s.a.w.) was created so perfectly that as if he had chosen every aspect of his being. Imagine now that before coming to Earth, we could select how our nose, lips, eyes, hair, and complexion would be. That would be amazing. Many of us might even request a mirror in the womb just to see ourselves. Of course, this is a playful thought because there are no hairdressers in the womb!

The Prophet Muḥammad (s.a.w.) was created in such a way that he appeared perfect, as if he had chosen every detail of his being. His presence had a calming effect on those who saw him—reflecting the divine wisdom and grace with which he was created.

The One Who Luminates Like the Moon

We say that the Prophet Muḥammad (s.a.w.) was created free from any defect. This statement is very well described by Hassan ibn Thabit (r.a.). He said that:

خلقت مبرأ من كل عيب

You have been created free from every defect

When you look at the Prophet, it is so pleasant. They described his face for you and me, and they say:

وجهه كأنه قطعة قمر

His face was as though it was a piece of the moon

If you had gazed upon the Prophet Muḥammad (s.a.w.), you would have thought that he was illuminated by the gentle moonlight. His countenance was serene and beautiful, a true manifestation of Allah's perfect creation. From the very beginning, he was devoid of any bad qualities, and his character did not require any correction or rectification. He was known as the most truthful and trustworthy, often described as *Aṣṣadiqal-Amin* in Arabic, signifying someone who was completely honest and reliable.

This innate honesty and trustworthiness were crucial because he was chosen to convey a divine message. If he lacked these qualities, there would be no purpose in selecting him for this mission. And so even before he was a prophet, the people of his society recognised him for these virtues. They always acknowledged his honesty and trustworthiness.

One of his companions wisely noted that "if this man never lied to us about mundane worldly matters, he would certainly never lie to us about divine matters". However, as soon as he revealed the divine message, some people who did not know him well, immediately labelled him a liar. Those who knew him intimately, on the other hand, believed in him without hesitation.

This illustrates a fundamental principle that persists to this day: when you truly understand and recognise the character of the Prophet

Muḥammad (s.a.w.), you will unquestionably acknowledge his truthfulness. On the contrary, if you fail to recognise him, you may hesitate and delay in accepting his message. This reflection serves as a reminder to give him a fair chance and a genuine attempt to understand his message.

I want to share an example with you. I mentioned Khalid Ibn Al-Walid earlier, right? He claimed that the Prophet (s.a.w.) was protected. Now, let me tell you about ʿAbdullah ibn Salam, a companion who had been a Jewish Rabbi. In Madinah al-Munawwarah, they were waiting for the arrival of the Prophet Muḥammad (s.a.w.). When he finally arrived, ʿAbdullah ibn Salam stood on his toes to get a glimpse of the Prophet (s.a.w.) because there were so many people around him.

As he looked at the Prophet's face, he said, "As soon as I saw his face, I knew that this is not the face of a liar." It was a face filled with honour, dignity, and honesty. Sometimes, when you see a face, you just know that it is not the face of a liar. The demeanour and presence of the Prophet Muḥammad (s.a.w.) were truly remarkable. And then ʿAbdullah ibn Salam heard the first words come out of the mouth of the Prophet Muḥammad (s.a.w.). It is narrated in the hadith below:

ʿAbdullah bin Salam said:

> "When the Prophet (s.a.w.) came to al-Madinah, the people rushed to meet him, and it was said: 'The Messenger of Allah (s.a.w.) has come! The Messenger of Allah (s.a.w.) has come! The Messenger of Allah (s.a.w.) has come!' Three times. I came with the people to see him, and when I saw his face clearly, I knew that his face was not the face of a liar. The first thing I heard him say was when he said: 'O' people! Spread (the greeting of) *Salam*, feed others, uphold the ties of kinship, and pray during the night when people are sleeping, and you will enter Paradise with *Salam*."
>
> (Sunan ibn Majah 3251)

And so, afterwards this Jewish Rabbi goes to the Prophet and says: "I know this is the truth." He went to the messenger and said "I bear witness that you're a messenger (s.a.w.). You are the messenger we were waiting for." He made the declaration of the faith as he recognised that the Prophet was indeed the true messenger.

The Prophet's Life: A Pathway to Understanding Islam

When people express their desire to learn about Islam and ask me for a copy of the Qur'an, it is commendable. However, as a suggested point of entry, I often recommend starting with the biography of the Prophet Muḥammad (s.a.w.), known as the *sirah*. Understanding the life and character of the man whom Allah chose to deliver the message provides valuable context. By familiarising yourself with his story, you can approach the Qur'an with greater insight and appreciation.

It is not wrong to dive directly into the Qur'an, and I'm more than willing to provide you with a copy. However, I often recommend reading a book on the *sirah* first, as it can serve as a helpful foundation. For individuals who are new to Islam or those seeking to deepen their understanding—starting with the life of the Prophet can answer many initial questions and set the stage for a more profound engagement with the Qur'an.

Additionally, it is worth noting that the Qur'an was revealed in a specific order. The early chapters were revealed in Makkah and tend to be shorter, while the later chapters that were revealed in Madinah are more extensive and provide guidance on various aspects of life. Learning the Qur'an in this order can help clarify the historical context and progression of the message. May Allah guide us all on our path to knowledge and understanding.

Miracles and Blessings in Nature: Connecting with the Prophet

The miracles of Prophet Muḥammad (s.a.w.) are extensive. The animals as well as other creatures of Allah spoke and communicated with him. Trees provided shade for him by bending their branches, and clouds too would come to offer him shade. The Prophet Muḥammad (s.a.w.) experienced many miracles and blessings from nature.

For instance, there is a reference to Masjidil Ghamamah, which means "the Mosque of the Clouds." It was named after the occasions when clouds would naturally cover the area. The mosque was established on a site where people used to gather for the Eid prayer outside of Madinah. Even though it would be sunny and hot, the clouds would provide shade during these gatherings. This phenomenon is a testament to the blessings bestowed upon the Prophet Muḥammad (s.a.w.).

In addition, during the Battle of the Trench (or the Battle of Aḥzab) another amazing phenomenon occurred. In this battle, a trench was dug around Madinah as a defensive measure. The climax of this war was marked by strong winds and a storm that Allah caused to come and aid the Muslims—which helped bring an end to the battle. The natural elements seemed to align with the Prophet's cause.

Allah (s.w.t.) says:

...فَأَرْسَلْنَا عَلَيْهِمْ رِيحًا وَجُنُودًا لَّمْ تَرَوْهَا ۚ... ﴿٩﴾

...and We sent upon them a wind and armies [of angels] you did not see...

(Surah al-Aḥzab, 33:9)

In Surah al-Aḥzab, Allah (s.w.t.) recounts an incident when He sent a powerful wind and unseen armies of angels to confront the enemies of the Prophet (s.a.w.). Allah asks, "Do you not remember the time when We sent against your enemies the wind? And We sent an army of angels whom you could not see." This divine intervention was a gift from Allah, where a powerful wind and the assistance of angels were sent to aid the Prophet and his companions.

This remarkable event showcases just one of the many miracles attributed to the Prophet Muḥammad (s.a.w.). Miracles surrounded his life from a young age. In fact, he once mentioned that there was a stone in Makkah that used to greet him with "*Assalamu ʿalaikum*" (peace be upon you) before he received prophethood. It is mentioned in the hadith below:

Jabir b. Samura reported the Prophet (s.a.w.) as saying:

> "I recognise the stone in Makkah which used to pay me salutations before my advent as a Prophet, and I recognise that even now."
>
> (Ṣaḥiḥ Muslim 2277)

A curious young man once asked me if we could identify the location of that stone today. The response was that even if we could find it, the stone would not greet us as it did to the Prophet, as this was a unique blessing bestowed upon him by Allah (s.w.t.).

The life of the Prophet Muḥammad (s.a.w.) was filled with numerous miracles that attested to his prophethood. These miracles began from his birth and continued throughout his life. Some of these remarkable occurrences are documented in the hadith literature.

One early incident took place when he was a child and was entrusted to Halimah as-Saʿdiyah, his wet nurse. Under her care, their livestock experienced a significant increase in milk production, and their previously ill donkey became healthy and outpaced the others. This was seen as a divine blessing accompanying the young Muḥammad (s.a.w.).

As the Prophet (s.a.w.) grew, more miraculous events were attributed to him. There are accounts of the earth seemingly crumpling beneath him as he walked, allowing him to cover more ground with each step. During battles, he could mount a horse without a saddle and still outpace others. These were perceived as signs of his exceptional status, with even animals recognising his noble presence.

Another miracle recorded in both the Qur'an and hadith was the splitting of the moon. When the Quraysh—the Prophet's opponents, repeatedly demanded a sign, he pointed to the moon.

ٱقْتَرَبَتِ ٱلسَّاعَةُ وَٱنشَقَّ ٱلْقَمَرُ ١

The Hour has come near, and the moon has split [in two].

(Surah al-Qamar, 54:1)

The problem is, Allah (s.w.t.) says:

وَإِن يَرَوْا۟ ءَايَةً يُعْرِضُوا۟ وَيَقُولُوا۟ سِحْرٌ مُّسْتَمِرٌّ ٢

And if they see a sign [i.e., miracle], they turn away and say, "Passing magic."

(Surah al-Qamar, 54:2)

Indeed, the Qur'an acknowledges that some people, when presented with clear signs or miracles, still choose to dismiss them as mere illusions or magic. This stubborn refusal to accept the truth can be attributed to various factors, including arrogance, preconceived biases, or a desire to maintain the status quo.

However, despite their initial scepticism or rejection of these signs, many individuals who witnessed the Prophet Muḥammad's miracles eventually embraced Islam. The undeniable truth of these miracles, coupled with the sincerity of the Prophet's message, eventually led them to recognise the divine nature of his mission. This transformation underscores the power of guidance and the ability of people to change their beliefs and embrace the truth when it becomes apparent to them.

Chapter 5

Balancing Spirituality in Modern Comforts

Prophet Muḥammad and Worldly Comforts

The Prophet Muḥammad (s.a.w.) lived in a time very different from our own—a time when advanced technology and modern conveniences like the Internet, phones, electricity, and advanced transportation did not exist. Despite the absence of these technological advancements, the Prophet's life was marked by extraordinary divine blessings and an unparalleled connection with Allah.

In contemporary times, many of us are surrounded by a plethora of technological luxuries, which, while convenient, can often become distractions from our spiritual duties. As individuals grow older or experience life-changing events such as loss or realisations—they may find themselves increasingly drawn to a deeper connection with their faith and a more meaningful relationship with Allah.

It is also important to remember that the Prophet Muḥammad (s.a.w.) was not given these technological advancements because they hold no value in the eyes of Allah. Rather, these comforts, while they have their place, can easily become distractions, leading individuals away from their faith. Therefore, it is vital to focus on the substance of one's relationship with Allah and their faith rather than being solely consumed by modern conveniences.

The reminder here is that we should not let these distractions prevent us from fulfilling our religious obligations, such as daily prayers and other acts of worship. It is crucial to prioritise our faith and maintain a connection with Allah—as well as recognising that comfort and convenience are not the essence of a fulfilling and meaningful life.

Material possessions and technological advancements in this world hold little value in the sight of Allah. They are like the wing of a fly compared to the vastness of His creation. While technology and the conveniences of modern life can be useful, they can also be distractions if we misuse them.

Embracing technology and modern amenities is not the issue; it is how we use them that matters. For example, having a smartphone or a comfortable bed is not inherently problematic. However, if we allow these conveniences to prevent us from fulfilling our religious duties, such as not waking up for *Fajr* prayer, then they become distractions.

The story of the Prophet Muḥammad (s.a.w.) serves as a powerful example. Despite being the greatest of all mankind and a true messenger of Allah, he led a simple life. When the disbelievers challenged him, saying that if he were a prophet, he should have had gardens, castles, and luxuries—the Prophet Muḥammad (s.a.w.) maintained his dedication to Allah's message and lived a humble and modest life.

In essence, the message is to use technology and worldly comforts wisely, not allowing them to distract us from our faith and religious obligations. Material wealth and technology should never compromise our devotion to Allah, as our relationship with Him is the most valuable and significant aspect of our lives.

تَبَارَكَ ٱلَّذِىٓ إِن شَآءَ جَعَلَ لَكَ خَيْرًا مِّن ذَٰلِكَ جَنَّـٰتٍ
تَجْرِى مِن تَحْتِهَا ٱلْأَنْهَـٰرُ وَيَجْعَل لَّكَ قُصُورًا ﴿١٠﴾

Blessed is He who, if He willed, could have made for you [something] better than that—gardens beneath which rivers flow—and could make for you palaces.

(Surah al-Furqan, 25:10)

Allah reminds us in the Qur'an that if He willed, He could have given us something far better than the material blessings of this world, such as gardens with flowing rivers and palaces. However, Allah has chosen something even greater for us—*Jannah*.

This verse emphasises that the challenges, struggles, and difficulties we face on Earth are opportunities for us to draw closer to Allah and earn our place in paradise. Instead of viewing hardships and trials as negative experiences, we should see them as opportunities for growth and opportunities to earn Allah's mercy.

Allah (s.w.t.) says:

وَلَسَوْفَ يُعْطِيكَ رَبُّكَ فَتَرْضَىٰٓ ﴿٥﴾

And your Lord is going to give you, and you will be satisfied.

(Surah aḍ-Ḍuḥa, 93:5)

I want to share something remarkable about the above verse in Surah aḍ-Ḍuḥa. While it addresses the Prophet Muḥammad (s.a.w.), the message is applicable to all of us. Allah says, "Very soon, We will give you until you are pleased," referring to the letter "ف" (fa) in the word "فَتَرْضَى".

I have come across various translations of this verse. Many translate it as "So you will be pleased" or "So you will be happy." However, the "fa" in "فَتَرْضَى" signifies a continuous process, suggesting **until** you will be pleased. In essence, it means that Allah will keep giving you until you reach a point of satisfaction and contentment.

Additionally, often in our lives, we face challenging times and difficulties, such as job problems, family issues, health concerns, or various other issues like marriage or the well-being of our children. It is important to remember that these trials are not punishments from Allah, especially if you continually seek His forgiveness. As a believer who sincerely seeks forgiveness, there is no reason for Allah to be upset with you.

Allah explicitly states that He does not punish those who are actively seeking His forgiveness. Instead, these trials and challenges are tests from Allah. They are opportunities for personal growth and development. When you face adversity, it is a reminder from Allah that He has not abandoned or forgotten you. Instead, He is merely polishing you to emerge as a better and more resilient individual.

Sometimes, people do not make positive changes in their lives until they encounter challenges. A near-death experience, for instance, can serve as a wake-up call, prompting a person to reevaluate their life and priorities. These experiences remind us to turn back to Allah and prepare for the Hereafter.

Imagine now that you have had a close brush with death, and then you find yourself on the other side. You might meet people who have already passed away. It is a profound experience. On Earth, you may tell others, "I almost died," because you survived. However, when you pass away and transition to the other side, you will likely meet those who have already passed. There, you won't be saying, "I almost died." You will simply acknowledge, "I am here, *SubḥānAllāh*."

May Allah grant us goodness and may He bestow his forgiveness to us all.

Reflecting on the Magnificence of Creation

The creation of the heavens and the Earth, or the skies and the Earth, far surpasses the creation of humanity in terms of grandeur and significance. In comparison, human beings are indeed quite insignificant. If we reflect upon the marvels of our own creations, we can truly appreciate the mind-boggling achievements of humankind.

In times long past, when people gazed at the sky, they were filled with awe, exclaiming "*SubḥānAllāh*" as they marvelled at the magnificence of the celestial expanse. During the evenings, the sight of the moon and stars left them in wonder, uttering, "Wow, *SubḥānAllāh*," as they contemplated the divine creation of Allah.

Believers, in particular, were keen to observe the heavens and the vastness of the Earth, acknowledging the immense size and intricacies of the world. Their reverence for Allah's creation deepened as they contemplate the vastness and complexity of the universe.

Today, we have an incredible technological marvel known as the James Webb Telescope. Have you heard of it? If not, I encourage you to look it up, download the app, and start following its updates. This telescope was launched into space, positioned approximately one million kilometres away from Earth or possibly even farther. Find out its precise location right now and observe what it is capturing.

In real-time, as I speak to you, the James Webb Telescope is making groundbreaking discoveries. It is revealing thousands and even millions of massive planets. They are sending back images that you can view on your phone or any device with internet access. It is not just planets; they have also stumbled upon galaxies. Gone are the days when we merely talked about Venus, Pluto, or Mars—these recent discoveries are on an entirely different scale. Galaxies upon galaxies have been unveiled, and it is happening right now.

Reflect on this for a moment. Imagine seeing these countless planets and galaxies, and you will find yourself exclaiming, "*SubḥānAllāh.*" How can anyone remain in doubt? When all of humanity learns about this and begins to comprehend it, they will have no choice but to acknowledge the existence of a Creator.

The Last Person to Enter Paradise: A Reward Beyond Comprehension

Let us remember a powerful hadith. The hadith says that the last person to enter Paradise will receive an inheritance equivalent to the Earth, multiplied by two, three, four, and even ten times. The sheer vastness of the cosmos makes you wonder, *SubḥānAllāh*, how will Allah grant me ten of these whole worlds for myself? While not necessarily the Earth, the equivalent of that, ten times over. Allah informs us that the last person to enter Paradise will be so overjoyed to be there that they won't ask for anything more. Simply being in Paradise is enough.

Reflect on our lives—if we are granted admission into Paradise, that is a tremendous blessing. It is a moment to be celebrated. In fact, just stepping inside would suffice. We are gathered here today at a venue called SACC. When the event tickets were made available, they sold out rapidly, with many eager attendees.

Now, consider this: we are talking about an event, a mere gathering. It is not Paradise. You can listen to the lectures later, perhaps a month from now. But *Jannah*, the real Paradise, will always be there—waiting. One day, it will be accessible to us, *inshā'Allāh*. If people are so enthusiastic to secure tickets for an event, imagine the eagerness to secure a spot in *Jannah*. Even if you are just at the entrance, as you approach the door, you will feel the goodness and a breeze of tranquillity. And you will realise, "I made it." Allah says that when you enter, you will be granted whatever you desire, even if it is just an entry.

Now that you made it inside, what if you were offered the whole Earth? Would that be enough? What if that was multiplied tenfold? You'd probably say, "That's more than sufficient."

Allah (s.w.t.) tells His servant, "For you, there are ten times what was on Earth." And this is for the last person to enter Paradise, the one considered the lowest among us. Now, imagine what awaits someone who's slightly better, let alone the rest of the believers. The greatness of this reward is beyond our comprehension.

So I tell myself, "I'm either going to be that last person, or someone better." If you consider yourself the worst, at least you will get that much. And if you are not the worst, you will be above that, *inshā'Allāh*. We hope and pray for Allah's grace. There is so much to look forward to.

Closing Thoughts and Prayer

In today's world, where we face uncertainties, anxieties, economic challenges, and global issues, it is essential to place our trust in Allah and leave our affairs in His hands. Allah is the Greatest, and through *sabr* and trust in Him, we can overcome any difficulties and find peace and success in this world and the Hereafter.

As our time together comes to an end, I pray that the words and knowledge shared in this book will inspire you to draw closer to the teachings and example of the Prophet Muḥammad (s.a.w.). It is essential to recognise and appreciate his profound value in our lives.

May you continue to seek knowledge, attend workshops, and engage in learning opportunities that bring you closer to Allah and His Messenger. Remember that the pursuit of beneficial knowledge is a path to paradise, and may Allah make your journey to *Jannah* easy and straightforward.

May Allah bless you all dear brothers and sisters, and may His guidance and mercy be with you on this path of understanding and growing closer to Him and His beloved Prophet. *Āmīn.*

Allah and I
Dr Muhammad Salah

Table of Content

Preface 115

Chapter 1: Establishing the Concept of *'Aqidah* 117

The Story of the Companions 118

Chapter 2: Allah is the *Waliyy* 121

Becoming His *Awliya'* 122

Nawafil and *Fard* 124

Chapter 3: When Allah Loves His Servants 128

Not Wanting to Be Recognised: Uways al-Qarani 131

Seeking the Pleasure of Allah (s.w.t.) 135

Chapter 4: Relationship with Allah 137

Loving Allah and His Enemies? 141

Chapter 5: The Sweetness of *Iman* 143

1.To love Allah and His Messenger more than anyone else. 145

2.Who loves a person and he loves him only for Allah's sake 148

Acquiring the Love of Allah 150

Ending Remarks 155

Preface

Throughout the Qur'an, the traditional teachings of our beloved Prophet Muḥammad (s.a.w.) and those who followed his footsteps generations later known as the concept of *ʿaqidah*, or the firm establishment of our beliefs—serve as the cornerstone upon which our spiritual journey is built. In the next few pages, I urge you all, the readers, to embark on a reflective exploration into the lives of those who embodied this essence and witness how the establishment of *ʿaqidah* in their lives have transformed their existence. Such are the likes of Anas ibn Malik and Rabiʿah ibn Kaʿb al-Aslami. May Allah be pleased with them as an example.

The best of all generations, the companions of the Prophet Muḥammad (s.a.w.) in particular, stand as radiant beacons in the history of human existence. Their unwavering commitment to the *din* of Allah (s.w.t.), their profound love for their Creator and His Messenger (s.a.w.), and their dedication to the main purpose of life which is worshipping Allah (s.w.t.) serve as timeless examples.

As we delve into the depths of Divine love, the love of Allah (s.w.t.) to His servant, we explore how the believers, through their actions and adherence to the values of the *din*, can attain the esteemed status of being Allah's *awliya'* or close allies of Allah (s.w.t.).

In the pages that follow, we traverse the landscapes of sincerity, discovering the humility of those like Uwais al-Qarni, who sought the pleasure of Allah (s.w.t.) in anonymity without rushing after worldly gains. Their stories resonate with the purity of intention, reminding all of us that recognition in the eyes of Allah (s.w.t.) far surpasses the hype surrounding the acknowledgement and appreciation of people for whatever we have done.

This section also sheds some light on the connection between *ʿaqidah*, actions, and the love of Allah (s.w.t.). We uncover the profound impact of Allah's love on the lives of individuals and explore the heights to which sincerity and devotion can elevate us. At the end of this section, we will discover that the establishment of *faraiḍ*—obligatory actions and *nawafil*—

optional deeds, become not merely a ritualistic practice, but a pathway to invoke Allah's love into our daily lives.

As we navigate these narratives and teachings by Allah's permission, we will also contemplate the profound wisdom encapsulated in seeking the pleasure of Allah (s.w.t.) throughout our day-to-day activities. Consequently, we experience the true sweetness of faith, we enhance our relationship with Allah (s.w.t.), and we clearly see how the transformative power of living a life grounded in obeying Allah (s.w.t.) awaits those who embark on this spiritual journey.

Dr Muhammad Salah

Chapter 1

Establishing the Concept of *'Aqidah*

The Story of the Companions

Anas ibn Malik (r.a.)

Anas ibn Malik (r.a.) was close to the Prophet (s.a.w.) so he was always together with the Prophet (s.a.w.). One day, once he and the Prophet (s.a.w.) finished the prayers, and they were leaving the masjid, a Badwin man stopped the Prophet (s.a.w.). Then, he asked them a question, he said, "O' Rasulullah, when is the Day of Judgment?" This question, by the way, has been asked multiple times not only to Prophet Muḥammad, but to all the Prophets before him, as a way of challenging the prophets. Some of them asked, "You claimed that there would be a life after death. There will be an eruption and reckonings. When is it? Bring it on." But the question this time was asked genuinely. This man really wanted to know, when will the Day of Resurrection take place. So the Prophet (s.a.w.) answered his question with another question, "You were asking about the Day of Judgment, what have you prepared for it?", so the man said, "I haven't done much of prayers and fasting, and charity, but for certain I love Allah and His Messenger." So the Prophet (s.a.w.) said to him immediately, "On the Day of Judgment, when it will take place, you will be gathered in the company of those whom you love." The Prophet (s.a.w.) assured him that on the Day of Judgment, he would be in the company of those whom he loves. Anas ibn Malik heard that and said, "By Allah, that was the best news ever, ever since we accepted Islam." And he used to say, "So I love the Messenger of Allah, I love Abu Bakr, I love 'Umar, and I really hope to be with them in *al-Firdaws al-A'la*, even though I didn't catch up with them, in doing good deeds, right his deeds and so on, but because of the merit of love in the righteous ones."

> "A man asked the Prophet (s.a.w.) about the Hour (i.e. Day of Judgment) saying, 'When will the Hour be?' The Prophet (s.a.w.) said, 'What have you prepared for it?' The man said, 'Nothing, except that I love Allah and His Apostle.' The Prophet (s.a.w.) said, 'You will be with those whom you love.' We had never been so glad as we were on hearing that saying of the Prophet (i.e., 'You will be with those whom you love.') Therefore, I love the Prophet, Abu Bakr and 'Umar, and I hope that I will be with them because of my love for them though my deeds are not similar to theirs."
>
> (Ṣaḥiḥ al-Bukhari 3688)

Rabiʿah Ibn Kaʿab al-Aslami (r.a.)

Another companion by the name Rabiʿah ibn Kaʿab al-Aslami (r.a.) was a very smart companion of the Prophet (s.a.w.). He used to voluntarily serve the Prophet (s.a.w) and he spent the night with him sometimes in order to put the ablution water for him whenever he would get up for *tahajjud* and so on. So the Prophet (s.a.w.) appreciated what he did so much he wanted to reward him. So one day he said, "O' Rabiʿah, tell me, ask from me, I want to reward you, I want to give you. What do you want?", so he said, 'Give me a chance to think.'

And every time I read or think of Rabiʿah ibn Kaʿab al-Aslami, I would say, "If I were him, I would say: I want to go to *Jannah*." But he was much more zealous than any of my thoughts. He said, 'O' Rasulullah, I want to be with you.' Where? 'In *Jannah*.' So the Prophet (s.a.w.) has already established in the minds of his companions and followers that he is only the Messenger of Allah. He does not distribute vouchers of salvation.

So he said, 'O' Rabiʿah, can I help you with anything else?' He goes, 'I do not own *Jannah* to say *inshā'Allāh*, you'll be with me.' And in his answer, he is establishing a very important concept of *ʿaqidah*. Because nowadays we hear people who distribute shares in heaven, and that is not true. So the Prophet (s.a.w.) said, "In order to be with me in Jannah, you have to help me out, you have to do something to deserve it, besides loving Allah and His Messenger, you have to prove it with كَثْرَةِ السُّجُودِ."

Rabiʿah b. Kaʿab said:

> I was with Allah's Messenger (s.a.w.) one night. and I brought him water and what he required. He said to me: Ask (anything you like). I said: I ask your company in Paradise. He (the Holy Prophet) said: Or anything else besides it. I said: That is all (what I require). He said: Then help me to achieve this for you by devoting yourself often to prostration.
>
> (Ṣaḥiḥ Muslim 489)

Kathir as-sujud means to offer a lot of prayers. This means not only the obligatory five daily prayers but also the *nawafil*; the optional, non-obligatory prayers.

أَلَا إِنَّ سِلْعَةَ اللَّهِ غَالِيَةٌ أَلَا إِنَّ سِلْعَةَ اللَّهِ الْجَنَّةُ

"Verily, the merchandise of Allah is valuable, surely the merchandise of Allah is Paradise."

(Jamiʿ at-Tirmidhi 2450)

Chapter 2

Allah is the *Waliyy*

Becoming His *Awliya'*

Indeed the commodity of Allah is very precious and expensive, if you want it, then you have to pay for it. It is none other than heaven. In this hadith, which was collected by Imam Bukhari, and it is narrated by the great companion, Abu Hurayrah (r.a.), the Prophet (s.a.w.) is quoting the Almighty Allah as saying the following. What did Allah the Almighty say in the hadith? He said:

...مَنْ عَادَى لِي وَلِيًّا فَقَدْ آذَنْتُهُ بِالْحَرْبِ...

Allah said, "I will declare war against him who shows hostility to a pious worshipper of Mine..."

(Ṣaḥiḥ al-Bukhari 6502)

Allah said "I shall declare war against anyone who showed hostility to any of My *awliya'*." An *awliya'* is a plural of *waliyy*, and Allah says in surah al-Baqarah:

ٱللَّهُ وَلِيُّ ٱلَّذِينَ ءَامَنُوا۟ يُخْرِجُهُم مِّنَ ٱلظُّلُمَٰتِ إِلَى ٱلنُّورِ ۖ وَٱلَّذِينَ كَفَرُوٓا۟ أَوْلِيَآؤُهُمُ ٱلطَّٰغُوتُ يُخْرِجُونَهُم مِّنَ ٱلنُّورِ إِلَى ٱلظُّلُمَٰتِ ۗ أُو۟لَٰٓئِكَ أَصْحَٰبُ ٱلنَّارِ ۖ هُمْ فِيهَا خَٰلِدُونَ ﴿٢٥٧﴾

Allah is the Ally of those who believe. He brings them out from darknesses into the light. And those who disbelieve—their allies are *ṭaghut*. They take them out of the light into darknesses. Those are the companions of the Fire; they will abide eternally therein.

(Surah al-Baqarah, 2:257)

Allah is the *waliyy*; is the Guardian, is the Guide, is the Friend, is the Supporter of the believers. He takes them out of the darkness into light. While the disbelievers; their *awliya'* are the *ṭaghut*, they rather take them out of light into darkness, such are the dwellers of Hellfire. May Allah protect us.

So the Almighty Allah says, 'Whoever shows hostility to any of My friends, any of My loved ones, any of My righteous servants, I shall declare war against them. Because he is annoying one of My beloved.'

Then, upon hearing that, a very certain you, one of the among *awliya'*, unfortunately in the mind of many people, *awliya'* of Allah is unreachable. They are kind of like ghosts, they are not like any of us. So let us learn what Allah the Almighty says in order to be among His *awliya'*, so He said:

...وَمَا تَقَرَّبَ إِلَيَّ عَبْدِي بِشَيْءٍ أَحَبَّ إِلَيَّ مِمَّا افْتَرَضْتُ عَلَيْهِ...

...My servant draws not near to Me with anything more loved by Me than the religious duties I have enjoined upon him...

(Hadith 25, 40 Hadith Qudsi)

Nawafil and *Farḍ*

There is nothing My servant can do in order to come closer to Me better than fulfilling what I have ordained upon him, which is any prayer of the five daily prayers is superior to the whole night prayer in *tahajjud*. This is *nafl*, but the *Fajr* is *farḍ*.

Oftenly when I went for *ḥajj* from the States, where people afford to go for *ḥajj* so many times—those who are going for the first time, they said, "Shaykh, I just came to check it out, but next time I will do better." They took it lightly, they landed at Jeddah airport and they said, "Shaykh, when are we going to do the *ihram*?" Too late. *Ihram* was done before you landed at the airport. But you are in big trouble, you have committed a big sin, which was *fidyah*, why didn't you ask? Why didn't you learn? You have been given classes. If you happen to perform *ḥajj* twenty times after the first time, it is not equivalent to the first time, because the first time is the *farḍ*. And what comes after that, is voluntary, is *nafl*. And Allah the Almighty says, "There is nothing My servant can do in order to come close to Me better than fulfilling what I have ordained upon him." *Wallāhi*, if you fast every other day, and you do not fast a single day during Ramadan deliberately without a proper reason, He will not accept it. Why? Because this is *farḍ*, those are *nafilah*; voluntary. Then He says, so this is every Muslim, every average Muslim must fulfil what Allah has ordained. We all have the same level, then He says:

> ...and My servant continues to draw near to Me with supererogatory works so that I shall love him...
>
> (Hadith 25, 40 Hadith Qudsi)

So you finish Ramadan, *alḥamdulillāh*. Next comes *Shawwal*. How many of you have fasted the six days in *Shawwal*? I assume many did not because they did not know it; after fasting for Ramadan, we happen to fast for six days in *Shawwal*, and the Almighty Allah will give a reward for fasting for the entire year. And if you do this on a regular basis, you will get the reward for fasting from day one until death. So the area of combination is *an-nawafil*, in giving in charity, go for *ḥajj* after your first *ḥajj*, multiple times in *'umrah*, and pray before and after the mandatory prayers.

Ummu Salamah, and Ummu Ḥabibah, have narrated that the Prophet (s.a.w.) has said:

> "If anyone prays in a day and a night twelve *rak'ah* voluntarily (supererogatory prayer), a house will be built from him in Paradise on account of these (*rak'ah*)."
>
> (Sunan ibn Majah 1140)

This means to pray four *rak'ah,* two before *Zuhr*, two after *Zuhr*, two after *Maghrib*, two after *'Isha'*, and two before *Fajr*.

As the Prophet (s.a.w.) has said:

رَكْعَتَا الْفَجْرِ خَيْرٌ مِنَ الدُّنْيَا وَمَا فِيهَا

> The two *rak'ah* at dawn are better than this world and what it contains.
>
> (Ṣaḥiḥ Muslim 725a)

These two *rak'ah* before *Fajr* are better than the whole world and all it contains and that is the sunnah. Imagine what would be the *farḍ* itself. So, these are *nawafil.*

The armour of the believer, whenever he communicates with Allah when people are asleep, Allah will communicate with him directly at night through *tahajjud*, the night prayer. So the area of *nawafil* is an area of competition to do more to come closer to Allah. And you will keep coming closer and closer, moving towards Allah until you have achieved the target. What is the target? *Ḥatta uḥibbah.* Allah the Almighty has already determined a certain target; to be loved by Him. Keep pushing yourself, striving harder, getting closer and closer, through offering *nawafil*; fasting every Monday and Thursday, giving a charity to the best of your ability, going for *'umrah* whenever you have some savings or chances, and praying at night. So when you hit the target, Allah will love you. What happens when Allah loves you? Many of us face difficulties in waking up for *Fajr* prayer. Even though they have set up their alarm, they still turn it off to go back to sleep. Once Allah loves you, you do not have to set up your alarm, you have a divine alarm to alert you. Not for *Fajr* prayer only, but way before that. Because you have a meeting with Allah, and some people don't.

So the Almighty Allah says:

...حَتَّى أُحِبَّهُ، فَإِذَا أَحْبَبْتُهُ، كُنْتُ سَمْعَهُ الَّذِي يَسْمَعُ بِهِ، وَبَصَرَهُ الَّذِي يُبْصِرُ بِهِ، وَيَدَهُ الَّتِي يَبْطِشُ بِهَا، وَرِجْلَهُ الَّتِي يَمْشِي بِهَا...

...When I love him I am his hearing with which he hears, his seeing with which he sees, his hand with which he strikes and his foot with which he walks...

(Hadith 25, 40 Hadith Qudsi)

What does it mean that Allah will become your hearing, your seeing, your hand, and your leg? This is obviously a metaphor, and it simply means that a weak servant like myself, when I bump into a beautiful woman in the mall, there are some sort of attractions I could not resist seeing. But when your sight belongs to Allah, even if the temptation is the greatest, you will not have any problem lowering your gaze—zero resistance. Why? Because Allah the Almighty is controlling your senses, everything in you is guided and guarded by the Almighty Allah. Your seeing, your hearing, your hand, and your feet are sitting with a group of people, and they start backbiting another person, who is absent. You are not going to be quiet like you used to be, saying that it is none of your business. Rather you say, "Brother, sister, I am so sorry, this is haram, you will offend them." Allah is controlling your hearing.

How much effort am I supposed to make in order to achieve this level? There is another hadith collected by Imam Bukhari, narrated by Anas ibn Malik, quoted by the Prophet (s.a.w.) in which the Almighty Allah says:

إِذَا تَقَـرَّبَ الْعَبْـدُ إِلَـيَّ شِـبْرًا تَقَرَّبْـتُ إِلَيْـهِ ذِرَاعًـا، وَإِذَا تَقَرَّبَ مِنِّي ذِرَاعًا تَقَرَّبْتُ مِنْـهُ بَاعًـا، وَإِذَا أَتَانِـي مَشْـيًا أَتَيْتُـهُ هَرْوَلَـةً

If My slave comes nearer to me for a span, I go nearer to him for a cubit; and if he comes nearer to Me for a cubit, I go nearer to him for the span of outstretched arms; and if he comes to Me walking, I go to him running.

(Ṣaḥiḥ al-Bukhari 7536)

Chapter 3

When Allah Loves His Servants

You need to show your effort, that you want it, then Allah will reward the effort twice. You need to show that you deserve it, in order to earn it. The Almighty Allah says, "Those who choose to be rightly guided, they take *shahadah*, they ask 'What am I supposed to do?'"

A brother is given an option to work for a conventional bank where he will be dealing with interest and haram, or somebody in a position where he is given a big lump sum of bribe, and say this is haram and resist it. That will be greatly and highly appreciated by the Almighty Allah. Then He will increase the level of your *iman*, and if you hit the target and you achieve the goal, and you become loved by Allah. Read this:

إِنَّ اللَّهَ إِذَا أَحَبَّ عَبْدًا دَعَا جِبْرِيلَ فَقَالَ إِنِّي أُحِبُّ فُلاَنًا فَأَحِبَّهُ - قَالَ - فَيُحِبُّهُ جِبْرِيلُ ثُمَّ يُنَادِي فِي السَّمَاءِ فَيَقُولُ إِنَّ اللَّهَ يُحِبُّ فُلاَنًا فَأَحِبُّوهُ . فَيُحِبُّهُ أَهْلُ السَّمَاءِ - قَالَ - ثُمَّ يُوضَعُ لَهُ الْقَبُولُ فِي الأَرْضِ...

When Allah loves a servant, He calls Gabriel and says: Verily, I love so and so; you should also love him, and then Gabriel begins to love him. Then he makes an announcement in heaven saying: Allah loves so and so and you also love him, and then the inhabitants of the Heaven (the Angels) also begin to love him and then there is conferred honour upon him in the earth;..."

(Ṣaḥiḥ Muslim 2637a)

When Allah loves any of His servants, He will tell Jibra'il (a.s.), and Jibra'il (a.s.) does not have to hear a word besides that, he will immediately fall in love with this person, then Jibra'il (a.s.) will immediately call upon all the angels in the heaven to inform them, so all of the dwellers of the *as-sama'* will love this person. Then he will be loved by the masses of people, even *wallāhi* by the non-believers. Why? They say, "*SubḥānAllāh*, there is *nur* on his face. I don't know his name, but *SubḥānAllāh*, despite his complexion,

I feel very comfortable around this person." They might not even know his name. And by the way, such people do not have to be admired in the community, do not have to occupy a high capacity in the community and as a matter of fact, most of the time they are being unrecognised, and they love it this way, and they want to keep it this way.

Not Wanting to Be Recognised: Uways al-Qarani

I am sure you heard about Uways al-Qarani. In reality, *al-waliyy* does not appear with a big turban and people are sitting touching his toes, or wiping his clothes. No, *al-waliyy* is afraid to be recognised, he only wants to be recognised by Almighty Allah. In surah Yunus, chapter number ten, verse number sixty-two and sixty-three, the Almighty Allah says:

أَلَآ إِنَّ أَوْلِيَآءَ ٱللَّهِ لَا خَوْفٌ عَلَيْهِمْ وَلَا هُمْ يَحْزَنُونَ ﴿٦٢﴾
ٱلَّذِينَ ءَامَنُوا۟ وَكَانُوا۟ يَتَّقُونَ ﴿٦٣﴾

> Unquestionably, [for] the allies of Allah there will be no fear concerning them, nor will they grieve—Those who believed and were fearing Allah.
>
> (Surah Yunus, 10:62-63)

Those who are being loved by Allah because of righteousness and piety. The word *'al-khawf'* means fear and al-huzn' means grief. *Al-khawf* normally happens in the past or the future, you are afraid of something that has happened in the past or is yet to come. When you say 'I'm afraid', what are you afraid of? The future. So Allah has already assured them with regards to the Hereafter. Don't worry about it, you will be saved. *Al-huzn* is when somebody is grieving; is sad about something that happened in the past or the future. **Don't worry about your family members, your loved ones, whom you will leave behind. We will take care of them because of you because you are a *waliyy*.** I want to be one of them. This hall could be full of *awliya'*, but we do not know about them enough that Allah has already knows about them. And He favours them, and He answered their *du'a'*.

So our friend; Uways al-Qarani was one of them. The term *ṣaḥabi* is considered an honour. It means a companion who happened to meet with the Prophet (s.a.w.) even once while he is a Muslim. Uways al-Qarani was one of those who accepted Islam, and he could have come to the Prophet (s.a.w.) to visit with him, and earn the title *ṣaḥabi*. He was living in Yaman, the Southern of the Peninsular. After a few days of travelling, he will be able to meet with the Prophet (s.a.w.), His most beloved. But he had an issue, he had an old mother and he was the only one to take care of her. Because of that, he favoured serving his mother. So Allah the Almighty loved him for that to the extent that his *du'a'* was made *mustajab*. In his supplications, whenever he says, "O' Allah", Allah will answer all his *du'a'*. And in the hadith, Allah says:

...وَإِنْ سَأَلَنِي لَأُعْطِيَنَّهُ، وَلَئِنْ اسْتَعَاذَنِي لَأُعِيذَنَّهُ،...

...Were he to ask [something] of Me, I would surely give it to him, and were he to ask Me for refuge, I would surely grant him it..."

(Hadith 25, 20 Hadith Qudsi)

Allah loves them, they are loved by Him. One day, the Prophet (s.a.w.) was sitting with Abu Bakr, 'Uthman, 'Ali, and all the chief companions. The Prophet said, "By the way, there is a person by the name Uways al-Qarani, he's from Yaman", and he is saying how much he is dutiful to his mother, and his *du'a'* is always answered to the extent that he was tested with a disease, it is called vitiligo or dyspigmentation—up until today there is no treatment for it. But when he said, "O' Allah, cure me, cure my entire body except a spot around my liver." So Allah restored his beautiful image, and said, "If any of you happen to meet with Uways al-Qarani, please beg him to pray for you, because his *du'a'* is *mustajab*." There is something missing here, the *du'a'* of those *ṣaḥabah* are already *mustajab*, and they are the best of the best, so who is Uways al-Qarani? He is no one, he did not even come to meet with you. But the *ṣaḥabah* keep that in their mind.

So when 'Umar ibn al-Khaṭṭab (r.a.) became the second caliph, every year he led the *ḥajj* caravan, and then he said, "Who's here from Yaman?" He kept on asking and asking, until one day he asked, "Do you have a person by the name Uways al-Qarani?" They said, "Yes. What did he do? Did he do something wrong?" for the *Amir al-mu'minin* recognised somebody so little. He said "I want to meet him." Then, Uways al-Qarani came, and when 'Umar ibn al-Khaṭṭab (r.a.) verified his identity, he said, "You used to have an old mother whom you used to take care of." He said, "Yes", "And were you afflicted with *al-baraṣ* (leper/leprosy), and you asked Allah to cure you except for a spot?", and he said, "Yes". 'Umar said, "I beg you to pray for me." 'Umar ibn al-Khaṭṭab (r.a.), whom the Qur'an was revealed four times to support his view, whom the Prophet (s.a.w.) said, "By Allah, if He is going to punish all of us, no one will be saved but 'Umar." 'Umar ibn al-Khaṭṭab who is the second in the list of the ten heaven-bound companion; begging somebody who is unknown to pray for him. Uways said, "O' *Amir al-Mu'minin*, I'd rather beg you to pray for me. You are the *Amir al-Mu'minin*." He said, "No, listen. We were sitting with the Prophet and he mentioned your name." "My name? I was unable to come to meet with him and earn the honour of being his companion, and he mentioned my name? How did he know?" "Allah informed him."

Allah said, "O' Jibril, I love Uways." So Jibril loves him. Jibril said to the angels, "Allah loves Uways," so they love him. Then he said to the Prophet (s.a.w.), "Allah loves Uways for the following qualities." So he loved him. And the entire ummah until the Day of Judgment love Uways al-Qarani, but only thirty per cent of us know about him. He is the true *waliyy*.

Tell me, what did he wear? What did he do? What did he look like? Look, none of that is significant. It is something between him and Allah. So Uways al-Qarani made *du'a'* for 'Umar ibn al-Khaṭṭab. Can you imagine? And then 'Umar ibn al-Khaṭṭab asked, "O' Uways, where are you heading after *ḥajj*?" He said, "I was planning to move to al-Kufa." Now the Muslim *ummah* has expanded, 'Umar ibn al-Khaṭṭab was ruling over two-thirds of the entire earth. And he was concerned about one person, not even to his own people. He asked, "What are you going to do?" He said, "I am going to write you a recommendation letter to the governor official of Iraq." So when Uways al-Qarani comes, the governor will take care of him, give him a nice house, a nice ride, a maid, and more. He said, "I beg you, O' *Amir al-mu'minin*, I don't want anyone to know about me." That is the true *waliyy*. People who have the urge to show off, there is no way that they are the *awliya'* of Allah. *Alḥamdulillāh*, one prayer at night is superior to praying during the day, because it is something that is between you and Allah. But when you keep praying at night, then you go in the morning with your red eyes, and you were hoping that somebody will ask you, "Are you okay? What is wrong?" "Oh, I was praying all night at home." *Lā 'ilāha 'illā-llāh.*

Two people entered the masjid, and they saw a young man praying. One of them said to the other, "*Mashā'Allāh*, look at the tranquillity, serenity of this young man." The other said, "*Wallāhi*, you are right, I have never seen anyone who is calmer in his prayer." The young man heard them, and he could not resist the urge, he looked at them and said, "And I'm fasting too." You want to be shaded with the shade that Allah the Almighty will give you, especially on the Day of Judgment. He said:

...وَرَجُلٌ تَصَدَّقَ بِصَدَقَةٍ فَأَخْفَاهَا حَتَّى لاَ تَعْلَمَ شِمَالُهُ مَا تُنْفِقُ يَمِينُهُ...

> "...a person who practises charity so secretly that his left hand does not know what his right hand has given (i.e. nobody knows how much he has given in charity)..."
>
> (Ṣaḥiḥ al-Bukhari 1423)

Somebody is doing it exclusively for Allah, does not care about anyone else, anything else it is for Allah's sake. And when people are upset:

> Verily, you will never leave anything for the sake of Allah Almighty but that Allah will replace it with something better for you.
>
> (Musnad Aḥmad 22565)

Seeking the Pleasure of Allah (s.w.t.)

If you give something up, even if it is tempting; even though you are broke, and you are walking on foot because you cannot afford a car, Allah (s.w.t.) will give you better than what you left for His sake. We have to seek the pleasure of Allah, even if that displeases other people. There was once this sister, she wanted to shake hands with me, she is the Prime Minister of somewhere, am I supposed to say, "Oops, I have to show the beautiful sight of Islam. I have to attract her to the *din*." What if she gets up to give you a hug and kiss? "Well I have to show her also that Muslims are very kind." No! 'A'ishah (r.a.) said that the Prophet (s.a.w.) never shook hands with a woman who was not lawful for him. He rather never touch a woman who is not lawful for him. I love the Prophet (s.a.w.), be like him. I do not care about whether the woman will be upset, Allah is going to be happy. And if He is happy, He is going to make everyone happy with you. They will appreciate that. It is not up to them, their hearts are being controlled by Allah. But on the other hand, when you are trying to please people even if that upsets Allah, Allah will be upset with you, and He will make those whom you have been trying to please on account of displeasing Him be displeased with you. What did you gain? Nothing. *lā ḥawlā walā quwwata illā billāh.* May Allah guide us with His blessings.

> "Whoever seeks Allah's pleasure by the people's wrath, Allah will suffice him from the people. And whoever seeks the people's pleasure by Allah's wrath, Allah will entrust him to the people. And Peace be upon you."
>
> (Jami' at-Tirmidhi 2414)

There is an *ayah* in the Qur'an, this *ayah*; number thirty-one, chapter three, surah Ali-'Imran, remember this *ayah*:

قُلْ إِن كُنتُمْ تُحِبُّونَ ٱللَّهَ فَٱتَّبِعُونِى يُحْبِبْكُمُ ٱللَّهُ
وَيَغْفِرْ لَكُمْ ذُنُوبَكُمْ ۗ وَٱللَّهُ غَفُورٌ رَّحِيمٌ ﴿٣١﴾

> "Say, O Muḥammad, 'If you should love Allah, then follow me, [so] Allah will love you and forgive you your sins. And Allah is Forgiving and Merciful.'"
>
> (Surah Ali-'Imran, 3:31)

This ayah is perceived by *as-Salaf. As-salaf* means *ṣaḥabah*; those who came before us, those who were praised by the Prophet (s.a.w.) when he said, "the best of people are my generation, my companions. Then the next generation; *at-tabi'in*, and the following generation, *tabi' at-tabi'in.*"

> "The Prophet (s.a.w.) said, "The best people are those of my generation, and then those who will come after them (the next generation), and then those who will come after them (i.e. the next generation)..."
>
> (Ṣaḥiḥ al-Bukhari 6429)

Chapter 4

Relationship with Allah

In this particular verse, Allah, the Almighty, has alluded to what the scholars of exegesis have recognised as *Ayatul Ikhtibar*, *Ayatul Imtiḥan*, or the verses of test. The test posed in this verse prompts a fundamental question: "Tell all your followers, and convey this message to the people of Madinah, including the Jews, Christians, and the hypocrites: If you truly love Allah, demonstrate it." This proposition is easier said than done. Many individuals claim to love Allah, yet they are mired in sinful activities and neglect their prayers. Therefore, it is essential to not just profess love for Allah but to validate it through one's actions.

This verse was revealed in response to the assertion of the Jews and Christians who claimed, "We are the children of Allah and His beloved." In response, Allah challenges them by asking, "Then why does He punish you for your sins?" This query serves to remind them that they are indeed human beings created by Allah. He forgives those whom He wills and punishes those whom He wills. The dominion of the heavens and the earth, as well as everything between them, belongs to Allah, and all things ultimately return to Him.

وَقَالَتِ ٱلْيَهُودُ وَٱلنَّصَٰرَىٰ نَحْنُ أَبْنَٰٓؤُا۟ ٱللَّهِ وَأَحِبَّٰٓؤُهُۥ ۚ قُلْ
فَلِمَ يُعَذِّبُكُم بِذُنُوبِكُم ۖ بَلْ أَنتُم بَشَرٌ مِّمَّنْ خَلَقَ ۚ يَغْفِرُ
لِمَن يَشَآءُ وَيُعَذِّبُ مَن يَشَآءُ ۚ وَلِلَّهِ مُلْكُ ٱلسَّمَٰوَٰتِ
وَٱلْأَرْضِ وَمَا بَيْنَهُمَا ۖ وَإِلَيْهِ ٱلْمَصِيرُ ١٨

"But the Jews and the Christians say, 'We are the children of Allah and His beloved.' Say, 'Then why does He punish you for your sins?' 'Rather, you are human beings from among those He has created.' He forgives whom He wills, and He punishes whom He wills. And to Allah belongs the dominion of the heavens and the earth and whatever is between them, and to Him is the [final] destination."

(Surah al-Ma'idah, 5:18)

Indeed, they asserted themselves as the chosen children and beloved ones of God. However, one must question the basis of such a claim and seek evidence to substantiate it. If they truly are the beloved of God, why does He then punish them for their sins? This apparent contradiction raises a fundamental question. In reality, they are no more than human beings, just like the rest of His creation, created by Allah. It is within His prerogative to punish or forgive as He deems fit. The dominion of the heavens and the earth, along with everything that lies in between, belongs solely to Allah, and ultimately, it is to Him that we all return.

In the context of discussing the concept of *waliyy*, the individual whom Allah loves holds a pivotal position, regardless of their personal inclinations.

I have a friend who once visited an elderly woman in a state of distress. He inquired, "What is troubling you, ma'am?" She responded, "*SubḥānAllāh*, I must have committed a grave error." My friend asked, "Why do you say that?" She explained, "Because I used to see him every night, but last night, he did not appear to me." Perplexed, he inquired, "Who are you referring to?" She replied, "Rasulullah (s.a.w.)." This remarkable woman, despite being illiterate, was blessed to witness the Prophet (s.a.w.) in her dreams every single night, and she was profoundly distressed by missing even one night's visit. It is a stark contrast to those who spend their nights engaged in inappropriate activities without any sense of remorse. It is challenging to fathom how someone like that could be beloved by Allah. A telltale sign of being loved by Allah is that your actions are guided and guarded by Him, and you strive to avoid displeasing Him.

Muhammad ibn Munkadir, who was born just a few decades after the Prophet's (s.a.w.) passing, once narrated a significant event. During a period of drought when the rain ceased for weeks and hunger and hardship prevailed, the people were instructed to pray *al-istisqa'*. The imam at Masjid Nabawi led these prayers, but there was no sign of rain. Sensing a problem, Muhammad ibn Munkadir recounted how he observed a man in the early hours of the morning, praying before the mosque's pillars. To his astonishment, this man made an unusual supplication, saying, "O' Allah, I swear by You, You must send down the rain!" What was remarkable was not his plea but his declaration, *aqsamtu 'alayk* (I swear by You). To everyone's amazement, despite the clear absence of any clouds in the sky, rain began to fall abundantly.

Intrigued by this mysterious man's connection with Allah, Muhammad ibn Munkadir decided to find out more. He discreetly followed the man after *Fajr*, tracing him to his home in the still-dark morning. When he knocked on the man's door during daylight hours, the man opened and inquired about his visitor's intent. Without a preamble, Muhammad asked, "What is your name?" Bewildered, the man questioned, "Why?" Muhammad candidly replied, "I overheard your conversation with Allah before *Fajr*." Startled, the shoemaker promptly fled and never returned to his house or his shop. His sudden departure was a clear realisation that someone had uncovered his profoundly intimate relationship with Allah (s.w.t.).

Loving Allah and His Enemies?

It is inconceivable to claim a deep love for Allah and His Messenger (s.a.w.) while harbouring affection for their enemies, fostering friendly relationships with those who harbour hatred for Islam and Muslims, or even those who have occupied Muslim lands and subjected our brothers and sisters to humiliation. Such love is, in essence, a facade.

In Surah al-Mujadilah, Allah explicitly states:

لَّا تَجِدُ قَوْمًا يُؤْمِنُونَ بِٱللَّهِ وَٱلْيَوْمِ ٱلْـَٔاخِرِ يُوَآدُّونَ مَنْ حَآدَّ ٱللَّهَ وَرَسُولَهُۥ وَلَوْ كَانُوٓا۟ ءَابَآءَهُمْ أَوْ أَبْنَآءَهُمْ أَوْ إِخْوَٰنَهُمْ أَوْ عَشِيرَتَهُمْ ۚ ...

"You will not find a people who believe in Allah and the Last Day having affection for those who oppose Allah and His Messenger, even if they were their fathers or their sons or their brothers or their kindred..."

(Surah al-Mujadilah, 58:22)

One cannot genuinely love Allah and simultaneously have warm relations with His enemies. It is an either-or scenario—you either love Allah or you love His enemies. You cannot love both simultaneously. As narrated in a hadith, the Prophet (s.a.w.) emphasised:

"...And whoever believes in Allah and the Last Day, then he is not to sit at a spread in which Khamr (intoxicants) is circulated."

(Jami' at-Tirmidhi 2801)

If you truly love Allah, if you believe in Allah and the Hereafter, and you anticipate the Day of Judgment when you will stand before Him for questioning, seeking salvation, you must avoid sitting with people who indulge in sinful activities like drinking. This does not mean you engage in such behaviour yourself. Rather, it signifies that you should not associate with individuals who openly defy Allah, despise His name, criticise His Prophet's Sunnah, and challenge His commands. How can you socialise with them, express affection for them, and claim to love Allah? Even if they happen to be your children, parents, or siblings, no one should take precedence over Allah and His Messenger in your heart and actions.

Chapter 5

The Sweetness of *Iman*

The Prophet (s.a.w.) has said:

> "Whoever possesses the following three qualities will have the sweetness (delight) of faith:
>
> 1. The one to whom Allah and His Apostle becomes dearer than anything else.
>
> 2. Who loves a person and he loves him only for Allah's sake.
>
> 3. Who hates to revert to Atheism (disbelief) as he hates to be thrown into the fire."
>
> (Ṣaḥiḥ al-Bukhari 16)

These three qualities; when possessed together, lead to experiencing the sweetness of *iman*. This notion might seem unusual—can *iman* actually have a taste? The answer is yes, and if you have not yet experienced that taste, it is unfortunate.

1.To love Allah and His Messenger more than anyone else.

But what does this mean? It means giving precedence to your love for Allah and valuing what the Messenger of Allah has said above your own self-love.

ʿUmar ibn al-Khaṭṭab (r.a.) had a son named ʿAbdullah ibn ʿUmar, who was an exceptionally obedient and devout individual. The Prophet (s.a.w.) held him in high regard and had immense affection for him. After the Prophet's (s.a.w.) passing, people would often see ʿAbdullah ibn ʿUmar from a distance and mistake him for the Prophet, thinking that he had come back to life. This was because ʿAbdullah ibn ʿUmar meticulously imitated the Prophet (s.a.w.), even in his manner of walking.

However, ʿAbdullah ibn ʿUmar once had a conversation with his father, where he asked something that could potentially hurt his feelings. He expressed his concern to his father, ʿUmar ibn al-Khaṭṭab, who was now the *Khalifah* of the Muslims, about why he always seemed to give preference to another young man over his own son. This young man was Usama ibn Zayd ibn Ḥarithah. Zayd ibn Ḥarithah was a man whom the Prophet (s.a.w.) had freed and declared him as his son.

So ʿAbdullah ibn ʿUmar asked, "Father, I've noticed that you consistently favour Usama over me, even though I am your own son. Why is that?" ʿUmar replied, "Son, know that Usama's father was dearer to the Prophet than even your own father. He was known as *Ḥibbu Rasulillah*, the beloved of the Messenger of Allah. Usama himself was also dearer to the Prophet than you were. I give preference to what the Prophet (s.a.w.) loved over what I personally love, even if it means favouring someone else, even if it's you."

This incident highlights the profound understanding of these noble companions of the Prophet (s.a.w.). They demonstrated their love for Allah by giving precedence to what Allah loved and what the Prophet (s.a.w.) loved. This principle of putting Allah's pleasure and the Prophet's guidance before personal inclinations is a profound way to earn the love and approval of the Almighty Allah.

فَلَا وَرَبِّكَ لَا يُؤْمِنُونَ حَتَّىٰ يُحَكِّمُوكَ فِيمَا شَجَرَ
بَيْنَهُمْ ثُمَّ لَا يَجِدُوا۟ فِىٓ أَنفُسِهِمْ حَرَجًا مِّمَّا قَضَيْتَ
وَيُسَلِّمُوا۟ تَسْلِيمًا ﴿٦٥﴾

But no, by your Lord, they will not [truly] believe until they make you, [O' Muḥammad], judge concerning that over which they dispute among themselves and then find within themselves no discomfort from what you have judged and submit in [full, willing] submission.

(Surah an-Nisa', 4:65)

Additionally, Allah has made it clear in the above verse that true belief requires something more than just acknowledging faith.In essence, this verse emphasises that genuine belief extends beyond mere words. It encompasses a willingness to accept the judgments and guidance of the Prophet Muḥammad (s.a.w.) in disputes and matters of faith. True belief means loving the sunnah, the practices and teachings of the Prophet (s.a.w.), and embracing them wholeheartedly. When you hear a hadith in which the Prophet (s.a.w.) conveys a sunnah, you should cherish it, aspire to follow it, and, if for some reason you cannot implement it, keep it in mind without criticising or mocking those who do. This respectful and loving attitude towards the sunnah reflects a sincere love for Allah and His Messenger (s.a.w.). It signifies that you honour the efforts of those who strive to follow the path of the Prophet (s.a.w.).

During my time at Al-Azhar University, I had the opportunity to visit another country, and there, I encountered a unique situation regarding cultural etiquette. The instruction provided was to use a knife with the right hand and eat with the left. However, in adherence to the sunnah, which advocates using the right hand for eating, I decided to go against the given advice.

In expressing my decision, I remarked, "I dislike doing that; I am going to eat with my right hand, following the sunnah." The response I received was a reminder of the cultural differences at play. The instructors emphasised that, due to the cultural norms in this particular country, it was customary to use the knife with the right hand and eat with the left.

In defiance, I humorously replied, "So what? Am I going to heaven?" This rhetorical question aimed to highlight the underlying principle that religious observance, such as adhering to the sunnah, takes precedence over cultural practices. The insistence to go against the sunnah and conform to local customs serves as a reminder of the challenges Muslims may face in upholding their religious principles in diverse cultural settings.

There is a narrated hadith by the Prophet (s.a.w.) addressing this very issue. The Prophet (s.a.w.) observed someone eating with their left hand. In response, he advised the individual, "Hey, use your right hand." However, the person insisted that they could not. The Prophet, known for his patience and gentle guidance, repeated this advice three times. Yet, despite the repeated counsel, the person maintained their refusal. Consequently, in response to the persistent rejection influenced by arrogance and ego, the Prophet (s.a.w.) supplicated, "May you never be able to use it."

> "A man ate in the presence of the Messenger of Allah (s.a.w.) with his left hand. He (s.a.w.) said, 'Eat with your right hand.' He said: 'I cannot.' Thereupon he (the Prophet (s.a.w.)) said, 'May you never be able to do that.' It was arrogance that prevented him from doing it, and he could not raise it (the right hand) up to his mouth afterwards."
>
> (Riyaḍ aṣ-Ṣaliḥin 612)

When you know it is a sunnah, you will love it, you want to do it. And if you cannot do it, you get others to do it. You do not criticise others who are following the sunnah of the Prophet (s.a.w.), and you claim that you love Allah, or you love the Messenger of Allah. That is not true.

2.Who loves a person and he loves him only for Allah's sake

The concept of loving for the sake of Allah is deeply rooted in the teachings of Islam. It signifies that when individuals serve the cause of Allah, embodying qualities and merits that align with His guidance, Allah reciprocates that love. It is a stark reminder of the importance of genuine devotion to Allah and choosing companionship wisely.

It is disheartening to witness when individuals express fervent admiration for worldly entities like bands or celebrities, neglecting the profound bonds that can be formed for the sake of Allah. On the Day of Judgment, when deeds are divided into two parts—good and bad—the sincerity of one's relationships will become evident.

ٱلْأَخِلَّآءُ يَوْمَئِذٍۭ بَعْضُهُمْ لِبَعْضٍ عَدُوٌّ إِلَّا ٱلْمُتَّقِينَ ﴿٦٧﴾

"Close friends, that Day, will be enemies to each other, except for the righteous"

(Surah az-Zukhruf, 43:67)

The Prophet Muḥammad (s.a.w.) underscored the significance of loving and hating for the sake of Allah, declaring it as the highest form of faith. The hadith states that perfect faith is achieved by loving and hating for Allah's sake, giving and withholding for Allah's sake (Sunan Abi Dawud 4681).

On the Day of Judgment, Allah will announce His love for those who loved, met, visited, and spent in charity for His sake:

> "My love is due to those who love one another for My sake, meet one another for My sake, visit one another for My sake, and spend in charity for My sake."

(Riyaḍ aṣ-Ṣaliḥin 382).

The special shade mentioned in the hadith for those who loved one another for Allah's sake symbolises divine protection and favour on a day when no other shade will exist. This highlights the eternal reward for sincere and selfless connections formed solely for the sake of Allah.

One day, the Prophet (s.a.w.) said to his companions, "On the Day of Judgment there will be some people that are neither prophets, nor martyrs. Yet, they will be envied by the prophets, martyrs, and the righteous ones; *ṣaḥabah*." This is because of their nearness to Allah, their honour to Allah. What kind of honour? Allah the Almighty will sit them on the right side of His arch, on pulpits which He created from light, and will cover their faces with lights. Who are they? The Prophet (s.a.w.) said, "They are ordinary people, they met and they love one another for the sake of Allah, even though they do not have any business relations, they are not blood-related." Recite this *ayah*:

اللَّهُمَّ إِنِّى أَسْئَلُكَ حُبَّكَ وَ حُبَّ مَنْ يُّحِبُّكَ وحُبَّ
عَمَلٍ يُّقَرِّبُ إِلى حُبِّكَ

"O' Allah! I ask You for Your Love, the love of those who love You, and deeds which will cause me to attain Your Love."

(Riyaḍ aṣ-Ṣaliḥin 1490)

When the Prophet (s.a.w.) was sitting, somebody passed by, and one of his *ṣaḥabah* said, "O' Rasulullah, I love this brother for the sake of Allah." The Prophet asked, "Did you tell him?" He said, "No." So the Prophet (s.a.w.) asked his *ṣaḥabah* to chase the man and tell him that "I love you for the sake of Allah." (Riyad as-Ṣaliḥin 385)

Whenever you love somebody for the sake of Allah, you should inform them. And whenever you tell somebody *uḥibbuka fillāh,* (I love you for the sake of Allah), their response should be *aḥḥabbakālladhi aḥbabtani fi,* (may the one whom they love me for His sake loves you as well).

Guess what? I love you for the sake of Allah. *Wallāhi*, I love you from the bottom of my heart.

And I ask Allah (s.w.t.) by the means of His love, to gather us in the right side of His throne and to put us on His pulpit be of pure light, to honour us because of loving one another for the sake of Allah (s.w.t.).

Acquiring the Love of Allah

Discussing the endless love for Allah and His Messenger (s.a.w.) is an ongoing and fulfilling journey. In the serenity and tranquillity provided by Allah (s.w.t.), sins are forgiven, as mentioned in a hadith. When people gather to learn about the faith, study the Quran, and praise Allah, they receive four special blessings. Tranquillity and peace fill the gathering, mercy embraces everyone, and unseen angels surround the assembly. Most importantly, Allah takes pride in those present, showcasing them before His angels, countering any doubts about creating beings causing mischief. He proudly points out, "Look at them, gathering from all corners to celebrate My praise and show love to Me." This divine acknowledgement is a remarkable privilege for those gathered.

There is a hadith narrated by Abu Hurayrah (r.a.) that beautifully illustrates the impact of such gatherings. When people assemble in the Houses of Allah to recite and learn the Book of Allah, tranquillity descends, mercy encompasses, angels surround, and Allah mentions them to those near Him. This emphasises the importance of collective learning and devotion, fostering an environment where Allah's blessings and acknowledgement flourish.

وَمَا اجْتَمَعَ قَوْمٌ فِي بَيْتٍ مِنْ بُيُوتِ اللَّهِ يَتْلُونَ
كِتَابَ اللَّهِ وَيَتَدَارَسُونَهُ بَيْنَهُمْ إِلاَّ حَفَّتْهُمُ الْمَلاَئِكَةُ
وَنَزَلَتْ عَلَيْهِمُ السَّكِينَةُ وَغَشِيَتْهُمُ الرَّحْمَةُ وَذَكَرَهُمُ
اللَّهُ فِيمَنْ عِنْدَ

"Any group of people that assemble in one of the Houses of Allah to recite the Book of Allah, learning and teaching it, tranquillity will descend upon them, mercy will engulf them, angels will surround them and Allah will make mention of them to those (the angels) in His proximity."

(Riyaḍ aṣ-Ṣaliḥin 1023)

In surah al-Ma'idah verse fifty-four, the Almighty Allah is showing us the traits of those whom He loves.

يَٰٓأَيُّهَا ٱلَّذِينَ ءَامَنُوا۟ مَن يَرْتَدَّ مِنكُمْ عَن دِينِهِۦ فَسَوْفَ يَأْتِى ٱللَّهُ بِقَوْمٍ يُحِبُّهُمْ وَيُحِبُّونَهُۥٓ أَذِلَّةٍ عَلَى ٱلْمُؤْمِنِينَ أَعِزَّةٍ عَلَى ٱلْكَٰفِرِينَ يُجَٰهِدُونَ فِى سَبِيلِ ٱللَّهِ وَلَا يَخَافُونَ لَوْمَةَ لَآئِمٍ ۚ ذَٰلِكَ فَضْلُ ٱللَّهِ يُؤْتِيهِ مَن يَشَآءُ ۚ وَٱللَّهُ وَٰسِعٌ عَلِيمٌ ﴿٥٤﴾

"O' you who have believed, whoever of you should revert from his religion—Allah will bring forth in place of them a people He will love and who will love Him who are humble toward the believers, strong against the disbelievers; they strive in the cause of Allah and do not fear the blame of a critic. That is the favour of Allah; He bestows it upon whom He wills. And Allah is all-Encompassing and Knowing."

(Surah al-Ma'idah, 5:54)

Allah is warning those who believe, that whoever converts from His religion and abandons Islam, Allah will bring about better people, and will replace them with better people. What would be their qualities and traits?

i. يُحِبُّهُمْ وَيُحِبُّونَهُۥٓ

This love is mutual. There is no way that Allah would love somebody whom He does not love. Or somebody who says I love Allah, and Allah does not love him in return. This love must be mutual.

ii. أَذِلَّةٍ عَلَى ٱلْمُؤْمِنِينَ أَعِزَّةٍ عَلَى ٱلْكَٰفِرِينَ

Look at the traits, when they deal with the believers, they are humble. They are very kind and lenient in dealing with the believers. But when dealing with the *kafirin*, they are very stern against them; the disbelievers.

iii. يُجَٰهِدُونَ فِى سَبِيلِ ٱللَّهِ وَلَا يَخَافُونَ لَوْمَةَ لَآئِمٍ

They struggle and strive for the sake of Allah. They fear no blame of a blamer, as long as it is for the sake of Allah (s.w.t.).

That is indeed the bounty of Allah that He grants to whomever He wants and indeed Allah is sufficient for all the needs of His servants fully aware of their needs.

When you ask yourself why do you love Allah so much? Not only because He has cultivated us, and bestowed countless blessings upon us, but also because He chooses us to be rightly guided.

There are a couple of *ayah* in the Qur'an in which the Almighty Allah said, "If you try to count the blessings of Allah upon you, you will never be able to keep record." Can anyone hold a pen and paper and count how many blessings Allah bestowed upon us? Impossible. I will give you one example: there was an old fellow, eighty years old. His children, *Mashā'Allāh*, one is a district attorney, and one is a big doctor. They all have big positions. All of a sudden, he was unable to go to the bathroom, he had urine retention. He goes to the bathroom, but he cannot leak; cannot urinate. And his bladder was about to explode. So when they rushed him to the ER, the doctor there inserted the catheter into the bladder, he felt relief. Then when his children came, everyone wanted to reward the doctor for helping their father. The father then started crying, he said, "*SubḥānAllāh*, for eighty years I have been urinating, not once have I said thank you. And because the doctor helped me to empty my bladder once, we cannot thank him enough." I am not talking about breathing, or the heartbeat, or the intellect, or us being able to move and function, I am talking about urinating and defecating; answering the call of nature.

So when we realised that, for example, when we were asleep and had the urge, we would just get up, go to the bathroom, and answer the call of nature and resume sleeping afterwards. This process happens multiple times. When do you think of ever saying *alḥamdulillāh*? Don't you think that He deserves your love because of the countless blessings that He has bestowed upon us? Yes.

The second means of acquiring the love of Allah and really loving the Almighty Allah, is learning about His beautiful names and attributes.

In the mind of most Muslims, they think that there are only ninety-nine names and attributes of Allah. But it is not right. His names and attributes are not ninety-nine, they are beyond count. We are talking about the traits of the Almighty Allah the Creator. What about ninety-nine names in the ḥadith? I will tell you the whole story, there is a beautiful *du'a'*. But before that, since now we have remember when we wake up at night from sleep, remember the Prophet (s.a.w.) said:

> "Whoever gets up at night and says: *'lā 'ilāha 'illā-llāh Waḥdahu lā Sharika lāhu al-mulk, wa lāhul ḥamd wahuwa 'ala kullishay'in qadir. Alḥamdulillāhi wa ṣubḥanallaāhi wa la 'ilāha 'illā-llāh wallāhu 'akbar wa lā ḥawla walā quwwata illā billāh.'* And then says, *Allāhummaghfirli*, Allah will remove your sins."
>
> (Ṣaḥiḥ al-Bukhari 1154)

When you say; *'lā 'ilāha 'illā-llāh Waḥdahu lā Sharika lāhu Lahu al-mulk, wa lāhul ḥamd wahuwa 'ala kullishai'in qadir. Alḥamdulillāhi wa ṣubḥanallaāhi wa la 'ilāha 'illā-llāh wallāhu 'akbar wa lā ḥawla walā quwwata illā billāh.'* (None has the right to be worshipped but Allah. He is the Only One and has no partners. For Him is the Kingdom and all the praises are due for Him. He is Omnipotent. All the praises are for Allah. All the glories are for Allah. And none has the right to be worshipped but Allah, And Allah is Great And there is neither Might nor Power Except with Allah), and then you continue with; *Allāhummaghfirli*, (O' Allah! Forgive me), then Allah will remove your sins. Why? Because you remembered Him when you were half asleep. Then if you were to make any *du'a'*, Allah will answer it. Why? Because, even when you are half asleep, you still remember Him. That is highly appreciated by the Almighty Allah.

The same goes for drinking, the Prophet (s.a.w.) also says:

> "Allah is pleased with His slave who says: '*Alḥamdulillāh* (praise be to Allah)' when he takes a morsel of food and drinks a draught of water."
>
> (Riyaḍ aṣ-Ṣaliḥin 1396)

Once you say *Alḥamdulillāh*, upon eating or drinking, Allah loves you. Why? Because you recognise that it is from Him. Sulayman (a.s.) once came and said, "O' Allah, teach me something to thank You with, You bestowed upon me all those blessings." Allah said, "You just did." He asked, "I just did? How?" Allah said, "By recognising that this is all from Me, this is how you give thanks to Me."

Other ways can be recognising that His countless blessings are upon you are beyond count, and you can never thank Him enough and by utilising them, in what is halal, you thank Allah (s.w.t.)

One very prominent sign that Allah loves you, there is a beautiful hadith that the Prophet (s.a.w.) said, "When Allah loves any of His servants, He will utilise him." Does Allah need anyone's help? No. But He will use him in order to bring him closer. And He will make him love what he is doing. He will guide him and make him love doing good deeds; assisting him in any good deeds. If you cannot do it yourself, assist, donate some of your time, help spread the information, learn something and share it with others. This is how Allah (s.w.t.) will make use of His you in a way that will please Allah (s.w.t.).

Ending Remarks

I talked about the many names and qualities of Allah, more than just ninety-nine. There is a special prayer that can help improve your mood and ease suffering. Some people spend a lot on therapists for what they think is depression, but the Prophet (s.a.w.) says reciting this prayer can make a positive difference.

For anxiety and sorrow

اَللَّهُمَّ إِنِّيْ عَبْدُكَ، ابْنُ عَبْدِكَ، ابْنُ أَمَتِكَ، نَاصِيَتِيْ بِيَدِكَ، مَاضٍ فِيَّ حُكْمُكَ، عَدْلٌ فِيَّ قَضَاؤُكَ، أَسْأَلُكَ بِكُلِّ اسْمٍ هُوَ لَكَ، سَمَّيْتَ بِهِ نَفْسَكَ، أَوْ أَنْزَلْتَهُ فِيْ كِتَابِكَ، أَوْ عَلَّمْتَهُ أَحَدًا مِنْ خَلْقِكَ، أَوِ اسْتَأْثَرْتَ بِهِ فِيْ عِلْمِ الْغَيْبِ عِنْدَكَ، أَنْ تَجْعَلَ الْقُرْآنَ رَبِيْعَ قَلْبِيْ، وَنُوْرَ صَدْرِيْ، وَجَلَاءَ حُزْنِيْ

اللَّهُمَّ ذَكِّرْنَا مِنْهُ مَا نَسِينَا وَعَلِّمْنَا مِنْهُ مَا جَهِلْنَا وَارْزُقْنَا تِلَاوَتَهُ ءَانَاءَ الَّيْلِ وَأَطْرَافَ النَّهَارِ

O' Allah, I am Your slave, and the son of Your male slave, and the son of your female slave. My forehead is in Your Hand (i.e. you have control over me). Your Judgement upon me is assured, and Your Decree concerning me is just. I ask You by every Name that You have named Yourself with, revealed in Your Book, taught any one of Your creation, or kept unto Yourself in the knowledge of the unseen that is with You, to make the Qur'an the spring of my heart, and the light of my chest, the banisher of my sadness.

O' Allah, remind us of it what we have forgotten, teach us of it what we are ignorant of, and grant us its recitation during the night and end of the day.

(Ḥiṣn al-Muslim 120)

The *du'a'* says, "O' Allah, I ask you by every name of Yours, that You have named Yourself with, or You revealed in any of Your books; the Tawrah, The Zabur, the Injil, or the Qur'an, or You taught it of any of Your creation, or and deemed that You have preserved in the knowledge of the unseen with You, that we have no clue about"; which is the vast majority of the name and attributes of Allah. So what we know about is only the ninety-nine names, but they are beyond that. The traits of Allah are unlimited as He is the Creator.

There was a *ṣaḥabi*, the Prophet (s.a.w.) sent him as a chief of an expedition, but the people had a problem with him. Every time he leads the prayer, whenever he recites surah al-Fatiḥah, if he recites al-Baqarah or al-Kauthar, or an-Nasr, but he would have to end them by reciting surah al-Ikhlas every *rak'ah*. When people complained, he said, "If you do not want it, then I am not going to lead the prayer." So when they returned, they complained to the Prophet (s.a.w.) because they thought that he was doing an innovation. So when the Prophet (s.a.w.) asked him, he answered, "O' Rasulullah, I love it, because it has the description of Allah, some of the traits and attributes of Allah." So the Prophet (s.a.w.) said, "Indeed, Allah loves you in return.", because of his love of the surah.

My beloved brothers and sisters, how could a person love Allah without knowing His names and attributes? *Wallāhi*, one of the greatest means of *taqwa* in the love of Allah, is to study the names and attributes of Allah. Maybe one day, *inshā'Allāh*, we will have a course to learn the names and attributes of Allah.

Tadabbur is thinking about Allah's traits; about the creations of Allah.

كِتَٰبٌ أَنزَلْنَٰهُ إِلَيْكَ مُبَٰرَكٌ لِّيَدَّبَّرُوٓا۟ ءَايَٰتِهِۦ وَلِيَتَذَكَّرَ
أُو۟لُوا۟ ٱلْأَلْبَٰبِ ﴿٢٩﴾

[This is] a blessed Book which We have revealed to you, [O' Muḥammad], that they might reflect upon its verses and that those of understanding would be reminded.

(Surah Ṣad, 38:29)

Allah revealed the Qur'an so that people would ponder over its verses, comprehend it, and enjoy it. Not only the sound, but the meaning as Allah is conversing with us. These are all the means of the many other means that will make us acquire the love of Allah, not to forget last but not the least, *du'a'*.

Make much of *du'a'*, especially in your sujud. Ask Allah (s.w.t.) to put His love in your heart. Because if He puts His love in your heart, then He will love you in return. And He does, then Jibra'il will automatically love you, and he does, then *alḥamdulillāh*, all the angels will fall in love with you, and if they do, then everyone will love you. Why? Because you are loved by Allah (s.w.t.).

Questions & Answers

Question 1: How do I stay humble and be reminded of Allah (s.w.t.) when I have sinned?

Mufti Menk:

Bismillāhirraḥmānirraḥīm.

I think what helps me is to always remember the origin of where I came from and the fact that before my birth—I was absolutely nothing. Allah Almighty says in the Qur'an:

أَوَلَمْ يَرَ ٱلْإِنسَٰنُ أَنَّا خَلَقْنَٰهُ مِن نُّطْفَةٍ فَإِذَا هُوَ خَصِيمٌ مُّبِينٌ ﴿٧٧﴾

Does man not consider that We created him from a [mere] sperm-drop—then at once he is a clear adversary?

(Surah Yasin, 36:77)

Allah Almighty created us from a droplet of semen, so who are we to argue or question about His creations? We are just one of His creations. Dear brothers and sisters, we will one day face death. Thus, be humble and have humility. This means that we have to remember exactly where we came from; and to remember the fact that Allah is in absolute control of every aspect of our existence. Remember as well that if we have blessings—it is from Allah (s.w.t.).

وَمَا بِكُم مِّن نِّعْمَةٍ فَمِنَ ٱللَّهِ ۖ ... ﴿٥٣﴾

Whatever blessings you have are from Allah…

(Surah an-Naḥl, 16:53)

Whatever favour that you have been bestowed with, it is only and solely from Allah (s.w.t.). He gave it to you, and He can snatch it away from you in a split moment.

Ponder on this, dear brothers and sisters: How many people in this *dunya* have had their lives turned upside down in just one second? Many. Sometimes we might be thinking, "Wow, I'm earning so much." But then the minute we lose our job, we end up losing everything as a result of that. In essence, Allah (s.w.t.) can turn our lives upside down in a split second. Therefore, remember to always worship Him and be grateful for the blessings He has bestowed upon us. Show gratitude to Allah (s.w.t.)

What does it mean to show gratitude to Allah? Showing gratitude to Allah is by obeying His instructions and staying away from His prohibitions. Additionally, a part of gratitude is also to utter the words:

اَللَّهُمَّ لَكَ الْحَمْدُ كُلُّهُ وَلَكَ الشُّكْرُ كُلُّهُ

Allāhumma lakal-ḥamdu kulluhu wa lakash-shukru kulluhu

O' Allah, for You alone is all praise. For You alone is all gratitude.

We have to praise and thank Allah. Furthermore, serving people—where you serve humanity—is also a way of showing gratitude. Thus, look out for those who have less than you; serve them, give them and you will then see how Allah (s.w.t.) will continue to bless you with humility.

Brothers and sisters, do not for a moment think that we are above anyone; do not think that we are a big figure and are more important than everybody else. We are just **one** of the servants who is trying to earn the pleasure of Allah (s.w.t.). Throughout our lives, we might be earning the pleasure of Allah alongside many other servants, but we don't know for how long the match will go on for us. Additionally, we don't know how the match will end; we don't know who will score near the end. If we are winning at the end of the match of our life, then it is good news. On the contrary, if we are losing in the end, if we are losing the pleasure of Allah, then it is a completely different story.

Let me give an example of this through football. Your football team is winning in the first half and the score gradually increases. The score is, 1-0, then 2-0, 3-0, and then 4-0. It is only **halfway** through the match. However, you are already excited, and you are now mocking and jeering at the opposition team. You know how the football fans are: everyone is laughing, joking and mocking the others whilst pretending they are already the winners. But hang on for a moment dear brothers and sisters because it is only halftime. Guess what happens after halftime? The scores suddenly change from 4-1, 4-2, 4-3 and then 4-4. The fans of the so-called original winners are crying now. The match now goes into overtime, extra time, and penalties. In the end, the unexpected happens. What do you think happens? The opposition team—the team that was losing in the beginning—wins. By how much did they win? That is not a concern, and it does not matter. The main thing is that the opposition team won. So, what happens to the laughter, scoffs and jeering that happened at the beginning? Was it worth it to behave in that manner? NO.

In a similar manner, but a higher example is that of the winner on the day of *qiyamah*. The winner is someone whom Allah (s.w.t.) alone knows. A hadith speaks about the *muflis* on the Day of Judgement—a person who loses everything. Do you know why he loses everything? Because when he was on Earth he belittled, scoffed, and gossiped about others. He was unjust and ate the wealth of people and so on. Hence, his good deeds were taken and given to someone else. It is narrated in the hadith below:

> Abu Hurayrah narrated that the Messenger of Allah (s.a.w) said:
>
> "Do you know who the bankrupt is?" They said: "O' Messenger of Allah (s.a.w.)! The bankrupt among us is the one who has no Dirham nor property." The Messenger of Allah (s.a.w) said: "The bankrupt in my *Ummah* is the one who comes with *ṣalah* and fasting and *zakah* on the Day of Judgement, but he comes having abused this one, falsely accusing that one, wrongfully consuming the wealth of this one, spilling the blood of that one, and beating this one. So he is seated, and this one is requited from his rewards. If his rewards are exhausted before the sins that he committed are requited, then some of their sins will be taken and cast upon him, then he will be cast into the Fire."
>
> (Jamiʿ at-Tirmidhi 2418)

What was the benefit of being haughty on Earth if eventually, it is going to bring us into a downfall? Nothing. There is no benefit at all. Therefore, remember to remain humble. May Allah Almighty grant us that humility and may Allah Almighty bless us and help us to help one another. May Allah (s.w.t.) grant us the best ending as well. *Ḥusnal khatimah* is something that we should continue to ask Allah as well. Remember:

If the ending is good, then we have won.

If the ending is bad, then we have none to blame besides ourselves.

Question 2: As we all know, Allah shows His love towards His servants by giving them trials. But what if the trial is too heavy for them and it makes them believe that Allah no longer loves them?

Dr Muhammad Salah:

إِذَا أَحَبَّ قَوْمًا ابْتَلاَهُمْ

When Allah loves a people He tests them.

In a hadith, the Rasulullah (s.a.w.) said:

> "The greatest reward comes with the greatest trial. When Allah loves a people He tests them. Whoever accepts that wins His pleasure but whoever is discontent with that earns His wrath."
>
> (Sunan ibn Majah 4031)

Whenever Allah Almighty loves His servants, He will test them.

Why will He test them?

Who was the most beloved and dearest to the Almighty Allah?

Who is the greatest man who ever walked the Earth? Rasulullah (s.a.w.).

Let us count quickly a few tests the Prophet (s.a.w.) has been through. If any of us have lost a child or two, we know that it is an extremely painful thing. There is a lot of grief when we lose our loved ones. For the Prophet (s.a.w.), all of his children with the exception of Faṭimah (r.a.), died during his lifetime and that is very painful.

SubḥānAllāh, the greatest man to ever walk the earth, at the time of his death, was suffering more than anyone else. He (s.a.w.) was having a fever—a fever that is doubled than the one experienced by an ordinary person.

ʿAbdullah ibn Masʿud (r.a.) narrated in the hadith below that when he entered upon the Prophet (s.a.w.) and put his hand on the Prophet's forehead it was really hot.

Narrated ʿAbdullah ibn Masʿud (r.a.):

> I visited Allah's Messenger (s.a.w.) while he was suffering from a high fever. I touched him with my hand and said, "O' Allah's Messenger (s.a.w.)! You have a high fever." Allah's Messenger (s.a.w.) said, "Yes, I have as much fever as two men of you have." I said, "Is it because you will get a double reward?" Allah's Messenger (s.a.w.) said, "Yes, no Muslim is afflicted with harm because of sickness or some other inconvenience, but that Allah will remove his sins for him as a tree sheds its leaves."
>
> (Ṣaḥiḥ al-Bukhari 5660)

Some people think that if Allah loves somebody, that person will be immune. The person will be wealthy, healthy, and won't be suffering any pain or encounter any hardship. This is not true. This is *dunya*. This is not *Jannah*. ʿAbdullah ibn Masʿud (r.a.) asked the Prophet in the hadith with regard to his suffering, "Is this because Allah wants to raise you into the highest rank on the Day of Judgement?". The Prophet said, "Yes, indeed."

And so, when Allah (s.w.t.) wants to do good to somebody, He will test them. Why? To remit his sins as mentioned by the Prophet (s.a.w.) in the above hadith. What if the person dies without having any sins like the Prophet (s.a.w.)? In that case, it is then to raise the person to the higher ranks. In another hadith, Rasulullah (s.a.w.) said:

> "On the Day of Judgement, when the people who were tried (in this world) are given their rewards, the people who were pardoned (in life), will wish that their skins had been cut off with scissors while they were in the world..."
>
> (Jamiʿ at-Tirmidhi 2402)

It is mentioned in the hadith by the Prophet (s.a.w.) that those who did not encounter any sickness or hardship in this *dunya* will wish on the Day of Judgement that they had. They would wish that after seeing the rank and position of those who have suffered immensely—those who are in *Jannah* and way high above them. The people who are in the lower ranks would wish that their bodies had been clipped with clippers in the *dunya*. Why?

Why would they wish such a thing? They wish such a thing in order to earn the same level and rank as those that have been tested tremendously in the *dunya*.

And so if you are a believer, then being tested and tried by Allah (s.w.t.) is for the good of yourself. Another hadith mentioned the following:

Suhaib reported that Allah's Messenger (s.a.w.) said:

> **"**Wondrous is the affair of a believer, as there is good for him in every matter; this is not the case for anyone but a believer. If he experiences pleasure, he thanks Allah and it is good for him. If he experiences harm, he shows patience and it is good for him.**"**
>
> (Ṣaḥiḥ Muslim 2999)

How excellent is the condition of a believer? He is always good in any condition.

If something good happens to him and he is grateful for it—then Allah (s.w.t.) is happy with him accordingly. If something bad happens to the believer such as the affliction of loss of a beloved person, the loss of property, money or sickness and the believer is patient—then that too is good for him. Nobody behaves in this way in either condition except a believer. *SubḥānAllāh,* isn't it enough to be recognized by Allah (s.w.t.). Allah says in the Qur'an:

...وَٱللَّهُ يُحِبُّ ٱلصَّٰبِرِينَ ﴿١٤٦﴾

...And Allah loves the steadfast.

(Surah Ali-'Imran, 3:146)

...إِنَّمَا يُوَفَّى ٱلصَّٰبِرُونَ أَجْرَهُم بِغَيْرِ حِسَابٍ ﴿١٠﴾

...Indeed, the patient will be given their reward without account [i.e., limit]."

(Surah az-Zumar, 39:10)

Allah Almighty says that the patient will be given their reward without account. Furthermore, Allah loves those who persevere. Thus, when you endure the calamities patiently, it is a sign that Allah loves you.

On the other hand, if you don't endure the trials, if you are not happy and are objecting then know this my brothers and sisters: number one, that is not going to change the condition. Disagreeing and objecting are not going to bring back your loved ones who have passed away—rather Allah (s.w.t.) will be upset with you and nobody wants this; nobody wants Allah to be upset with them. And so remember, the believer is always pleased with Allah's decree for them. Additionally, on a side note, I want to mention that fifty per cent of *iman* is patience. More than eighty times in the Qur'an, Allah mentions patience, as well as its merits and the word of those who endure calamities patiently. May Allah make us among them, *āmīn.*

Question 3: Is it OK to not like someone or hate someone and keep it to ourselves? This question is mainly in reference to family members who often hurt us.

Mufti Menk:

Bismillāhirraḥmānirraḥīm.

The word hate is generally quite a strong word. As much as we have feelings of dislike towards people—which is a human trait—we have to be careful that it does not get to a point where we do not fulfil the other parties' rights.

It is a human trait to have feelings of dislike. Sometimes we don't want to associate with certain people. However, in general as believers, we should be loving to one another. We should be caring for one another. We should be empowering one another. We should be assisting one another. In addition, we should also reach out to the degree of the fulfilment of the rights of everyone. A Muslim has greater rights, but remember the non-Muslims too have rights. We have to be kind towards them as well as it is their right to receive kindness as well. They too are human beings hence they deserve that kindness and right.

In life, we will have people who have hurt us. These people might have done something and we dislike the fact that they have done the act that causes us hurt and pain. Later, a time will come when they would do more of the act and that will cause us to be more distant with them. Consequently, we will then slowly begin to dislike them—the person—and not just the act. This is because as soon as we see them, all the pain, abuse, hurt, hate, difficulty and hardship will come right back at us. Those painful memories will flash in the mind once again. Hence, disliking them and wanting to stay away from that person is something that will inevitably happen. However, it should never be to a degree that we do not fulfil their rights. An example of one of their rights would be to respond to their *salam* when uttered. If they say "*Assalamu 'alaikum*", then we would have to respond to that *salam* with "*Walaikumsalam.*"

We might not want to go beyond that however this is the bare minimum we have to do. Perhaps, we might not want to go beyond it because we don't want to interact with someone who has hurt us over and over again. It is said in a hadith:

Narrated by Abu Hurayrah:

The Prophet (s.a.w.) said, "A believer is not stung twice (by something) out of one and the same hole."

(Ṣaḥiḥ al-Bukhari 6133)

A believer is not bitten from the same hole twice. A believer is not bitten by the same source twice. Hence, we try to be careful with that person by not interacting too much. We tend to keep a safe distance from them and doing this is OK. All of this is OK. However, sometimes when the ill feelings come to a point where it is uncontrollable, it will lead us to do something wrong. Allah says in the Qur'an:

... وَلَا يَجْرِمَنَّكُمْ شَنَـَٔانُ قَوْمٍ عَلَىٰٓ أَلَّا تَعْدِلُوا۟ ۚ ٱعْدِلُوا۟ هُوَ أَقْرَبُ لِلتَّقْوَىٰ ۖ ... ٨

...and do not let the hatred of a people prevent you from being just. Be just; that is nearer to righteousness...

(Surah al-Ma'idah, 5:8)

Do not let our hatred for a person turn us and make us unjust towards them. Instead, be just for indeed it is closer to piety and *taqwa*. We need to be just with our friends as well as our foes. Therefore, remember to not allow the dislike feelings take control over us; do not let it come to a point where it will result in us becoming sinful.

Question 4: What is the ruling regarding charity towards non-Muslims? Should you give charity to Muslims only? What is the difference between *ṣadaqah* and *zakah*?

Dr Muhammad Salah:

Every charity that is given away, whether it is alms which is compulsory or voluntary—is called a *ṣadaqah*. Almighty Allah named *az-zakah* in the following verse of the Qur'an:

﴿ إِنَّمَا ٱلصَّدَقَٰتُ لِلْفُقَرَآءِ وَٱلْمَسَٰكِينِ وَٱلْعَٰمِلِينَ
عَلَيْهَا وَٱلْمُؤَلَّفَةِ قُلُوبُهُمْ وَفِى ٱلرِّقَابِ وَٱلْغَٰرِمِينَ وَفِى
سَبِيلِ ٱللَّهِ وَٱبْنِ ٱلسَّبِيلِ ۖ فَرِيضَةً مِّنَ ٱللَّهِ ۗ وَٱللَّهُ عَلِيمٌ
حَكِيمٌ ﴿٦٠﴾

> Zakah expenditures are only for the poor and for the needy and for those employed for it and for bringing hearts together [for Islam] and for freeing captives [or slaves] and for those in debt and for the cause of Allah and for the [stranded] traveller—an obligation [imposed] by Allah. And Allah is Knowing and Wise.
>
> (Surah at-Tawbah, 9:60)

Allah (s.w.t.) mentions in this verse the eight categories that are eligible for the mandatory *zakah* and Allah named it *ṣadaqah*.

In a hadith, Ibn 'Umar says صَدَقَةُ الْفِطْرِ meaning *sadaqatul-fiṭr*. And so, the Prophet (s.a.w.) named *zakatul-fiṭr* as *ṣadaqah*.

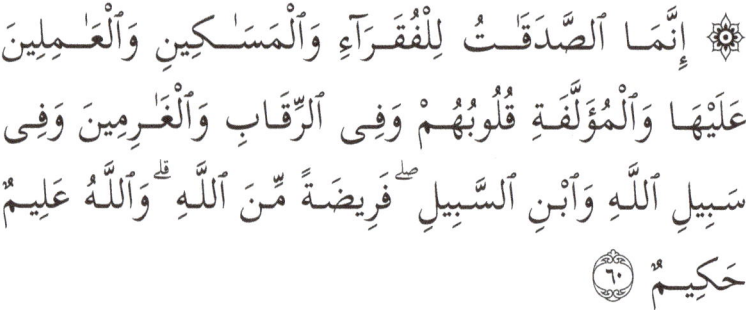

In essence, every *zakah* is a *ṣadaqah* **but** not every *ṣadaqah* is a *zakah*. This is because *ṣadaqah* covers the "voluntary charity" and the "mandatory charity." When it comes to **mandatory charity** such as *az-zakah* on one's wealth and position, the annual *zakah*, *zakatul mal* or *zakatul fiṭr*—it is exclusively for Muslims. However, the **voluntary charity**, whether you give it to the Muslims or the non-Muslims, you will be rewarded accordingly as you are putting it in Allah's hand. You will be rewarded accordingly by Allah (s.w.t.) based on your intention, sincerity and the source of income which is halal.

Let me give you an example. You have a neighbour who is going through an operation and people are raising funds for that person. He is not a Muslim perhaps even an atheist. However, you decide to support them financially and for that, you are rewarded by Allah. Why? Because you are not doing it for a person but you are doing it for the sake of Allah. Perhaps, you have a maid, a domestic helper a driver or just in general someone who is in need of help—and you decide to help them for the sake of Allah. With regard to these deeds, look closely at the following verses in Surah al-Insan:

وَيُطْعِمُونَ ٱلطَّعَامَ عَلَىٰ حُبِّهِۦ مِسْكِينًا وَيَتِيمًا وَأَسِيرًا ﴿٨﴾

إِنَّمَا نُطْعِمُكُمْ لِوَجْهِ ٱللَّهِ لَا نُرِيدُ مِنكُمْ جَزَآءً وَلَا شُكُورًا ﴿٩﴾

> And they give food in spite of love for it to the needy, the orphan, and the captive, [Saying], "We feed you only for the face [i.e., approval] of Allah. We wish not from you reward or gratitude.
>
> (Surah al-Insan, 76:8-9)

In Surah al-Insan, Almighty Allah mentions those who will be eligible to enter the gardens of Paradise—beneath which rivers are flowing. He (s.w.t.) said that it is for those who even feed the *miskin*, the *fakir* and the prisoners of war—those who came to fight us because we are believers, those who came to occupy our lands and we defeated them by the will of Allah and are now under our control. We don't put the prisoners of war in bunkers or in the ground. We do not starve them to death. Instead, we feed them from whatever we eat. Sometimes we give preferences to them over ourselves. As you can see, the verse above says—*"And they give food in spite of love for it"*— despite the fact that the people needed and wanted the food for themselves, they decided to give it to those who were in need. Why? So that when the prisoners say "Thank you so much. I really appreciate it. I didn't expect that", you can say that you too were not expecting a thanks in return. Instead, you were only doing for Allah; "*We feed you only for the face of Allah. We wish not from you reward or gratitude.*"

In addition, when you give charity to someone or anyone do not tell them or ask them to pray for you. Are you giving charity so that they can pay you back? NO. The verse above mentions—"*we wish not from you rewards or gratitude.*" The people who are on the receiving end will eventually pray for you. They will say "*Jazākhāllah khayr.*" And even if they don't, Allah (s.w.t) already did it, Allah has accepted your deed and has rewarded you.

Question 5: Hello. I am a convert and I have the opportunity to officially convert. However, it has to be done in secret and against my parents will as my mum was really angry when I told her about converting to Islam. I asked Allah (s.w.t.) that if my birthday falls on a Friday, I will convert. And, my birthday did end up falling on a Friday.

And so, my question is, is it bad to go against your parents for the sake of Allah (s.w.t.)?

Dr Muhammad Salah:

The Qur'an gives precedence to being obedient to the parents. It is to the extent that there is nothing that comes second to the commandment of *tawḥid* but being dutiful to one's parents. In Surah an-Nisa, Almighty Allah says the following:

﴿ وَٱعْبُدُوا۟ ٱللَّهَ وَلَا تُشْرِكُوا۟ بِهِۦ شَيْـًٔا ۖ وَبِٱلْوَٰلِدَيْنِ إِحْسَـٰنًا... ﴿٣٦﴾

Worship Allah and associate nothing with Him, and to parents do good...

(Surah an-Nisa, 4:36)

Worship Allah alone and be dutiful to the parents. Additionally, in another part of the Qur'an in Surah al-Isra', Allah says:

﴿ وَقَضَىٰ رَبُّكَ أَلَّا تَعْبُدُوٓا۟ إِلَّآ إِيَّاهُ وَبِٱلْوَٰلِدَيْنِ إِحْسَـٰنًا ۚ... ﴿٢٣﴾

And your Lord has decreed that you worship not except Him, and to parents, good treatment.

(Surah al-Isra', 17:23)

In essence, what comes after the commandment of *tawḥid* and worshipping Allah alone is being dutiful to one's parents. In another verse,

Allah Almighty says:

وَإِن جَٰهَدَاكَ عَلَىٰٓ أَن تُشْرِكَ بِى مَا لَيْسَ لَكَ بِهِۦ عِلْمٌ فَلَا تُطِعْهُمَا ۖ وَصَاحِبْهُمَا فِى ٱلدُّنْيَا مَعْرُوفًا ۖ وَٱتَّبِعْ سَبِيلَ مَنْ أَنَابَ إِلَىَّ ۚ ثُمَّ إِلَىَّ مَرْجِعُكُمْ فَأُنَبِّئُكُم بِمَا كُنتُمْ تَعْمَلُونَ ﴿١٥﴾

> But if they endeavour to make you associate with Me that of which you have no knowledge, do not obey them but accompany them in [this] world with appropriate kindness and follow the way of those who turn back to Me [in repentance]. Then to Me will be your return, and I will inform you about what you used to do.
>
> (Surah al-Luqman, 31:15)

In essence, if one's parents are non-Muslims, they are still commanded to look after their parents. They are commanded to take care of them and be obedient to them. However, what should they do if the parents are forcing and putting pressure on their child to change and give up on faith? For that, Allah Almighty in the above verse says فَلَا تُطِعْهُمَا meaning that it is the only condition where you are not allowed to obey or listen to your parents. Yet, afterwards, Allah says وَصَاحِبْهُمَا فِى ٱلدُّنْيَا مَعْرُوفًا. Allah says that the child still has to give the parents good company. The child has to take care of the parents' needs in regard to the *dunya*—money, healthcare services and so on. So, when the parents touch upon the matter of faith, the answer is NO to the parents, you are allowed to disobey them for that but you still have to fulfil your duty as a child to them.

This matter actually began at the time of Prophet Muḥammad (s.a.w.). Sa'd ibn Abi Waqqaṣ (r.a.) was one of the few people who accepted Islam early. Even before accepting Islam, he was a devoted son, especially to his mother. However, after he accepted Islam his mother, Hamnah bint Sufyan was in a rage and wanted him to leave Islam and return to Paganism. She vowed to not eat nor drink until her son left Islam. She told her son that she would not consume food and would rather die out of suffering and starvation

until her son abandoned Islam. Sa'd ibn Abi Waqqas tried to persuade his mother to eat and drink as he was determined to not leave Islam.

At one point he told his mother "Ya Ummah! You know how much I love you but know this ya Ummaah; whether you eat or you don't, whether you drink or you don't, whether you shower or you don't, I will not leave Islam." "Yaa Ummaah! Despite my strong love for you, my love for God and His Messenger is indeed stronger. By God, if you had a thousand souls and one soul after another were to depart, I would not abandon my religion for anything." In the end, she relented and started eating and drinking again.

Additionally, I have seen and heard lots of stories about children who when they revert, their parents accepted Islam after they saw changes in their child. These cases are happening a lot and I have seen this plenty of times. Let me give you an example of a case that I know of. A sister quit smoking after she accepted Islam; she also quit taking drugs and drinking. She became a completely different person. That change is contagious because the people around her looked at her and thought "I want to be like her as well." They too then change.

Another case I came across was about a brother who did not share with his family that he accepted Islam even until his deathbed. When he passed away, in his *waṣiyyah* he mentioned to his family members that he reverted to Islam and asked them to take him to the masjid, to the Muslim community so that he would be buried according to Islam. His mother fulfilled his *waṣiyyah*, his last wishes. Hence, instead of his whole family going to the church, they went to the masjid instead. When the Muslim community of that masjid received news that there would be a *ṣalah janazah*, many of them went even though it was a working day in Manhattan. When the brother's family saw a lot of people coming to the masjid to do the *janazah* prayers they thought that their son/brother had a lot of friends. But later they found out that these people were not his friends. They found out that nobody actually knew him. So, they asked the people, "Why did you come if you did not know him?". A man from the Muslim community answered, "We heard a Muslim has passed away, so we came to attend his funeral." The family was so impressed by how the Muslim community is adherent to each other. They were amazed at the love and respect the Muslim people had towards a man whom they did not know. It was so profound and mesmerising that thirteen of his family members took their *shahadah* on his funeral day. Thirteen, *subḥānAllāh*. Actions speak louder than words. Sometimes, we may give *daʿwah* by mere action, however, our behaviour as Muslims, and the way we apply Islam into our daily lives show people the beauty of Islam hence making them amazed to know more.

An interesting incident occurred to me in Virginia years ago. At that time, I was working with non-Muslims in a very prejudiced area. I was attending a meeting and the *ʿAṣr* prayer was during that time as well. So, one of my colleagues came up to me and asked "Muhammad how come you missed your prayer?" I was taken aback. I asked, "Prayer? How do you know about the prayer that I do?" She replied, "We people keep an eye on you. We see you. We notice you. We know exactly when you pray." During that time, I was working five days a week and my usual routine would be to grab my compass and prayer mat and then go to a private space to pray. It was just that on that day, during my usual time to pray my *ʿAṣr*, I had a meeting but I knew it was OK if I prayed later because I knew that the time for me to pray was extended till *Maghrib*. But of course, my colleague does not know that. But you see, our actions are being watched. I realised then that we don't actually live by ourselves only. And so, our behaviour as Muslims should be the greatest means of *daʿwah* and our parents are the most worthy to witness this beauty and change in our behaviour when we become a believer. The Prophet (s.a.w.) said in a hadith:

> "The Lord's pleasure is in the parent's pleasure, and the Lord's anger is in the parent's anger."
>
> (Jamiʿ at-Tirmidhi 1899)

To please Allah is to please your parents. I spoke about Uways al-Qarani during my section and I mentioned that even though he was not a companion, the Prophet (s.a.w.) asked his companions to please pray for him simply because he was dutiful to his mother.

Question 6: I want to get over a sin that I have been committing for the past 5 years but I am unable to. Every time I try to get out of it, I feel numb. And then I go back to doing it. Please guide me on how to get out of that sin.

Wael Ibrahim:

This question seems to be related to something that I do. The question is not straightforward however these are the types of messages that I do receive on a daily basis.

Basically, these hidden or secretive sins are destructive. They are not destructive for themselves being sinful and Allah (s.w.t.) punishing you for it on the day of Judgement, but they have a ripple effect that can actually destroy every good area in your life. For instance, it can impact your relationship with your spouse. It can impact your sexual performance and your intimacy with your spouse. It can impact your mental health. I have even released a book regarding this topic. The title of the book is *Porn is Mental*. It is about the mental health crisis caused by porn consumption, and it is completely from a scientific perspective rather than an Islamic perspective.

And so, in order for you to get out of those addictive sins—sins of that nature, you need to have multiple solutions and choices. You need multiple solutions in order for you to cope with the challenges.

An example of one of the solutions is environmental invasion whereby you have to cleanse your environment to be conducive to *iman*-driven activities; and being productive in *iman*-driven activities. The thing is environments fuel our behaviours. Imagine yourself sitting in the Kabah alone. You are just by yourself. In that situation, will you dare take out your cell phone and watch something haram? No. Why? Because the environment is so holy it encourages you to do something different, something better. Thus, number one, you have to cleanse your environment so that as soon as you are in any place, you will do that which is good and pure *inshā'Allāh*. Let me give you an example. For instance, don't ever take your Internet devices into the bedrooms. To those parents who have given their children cell phones and iPads, go check on your children's devices. You know what I mean by this. And so, whenever you head to your bedroom remember that it is for sleeping. It is not for the internet, not for you to lie down and scroll your life away.

Number two have a structured system; a life to live by and make sure you are dead serious about it. When the Prophet Muḥammad (s.a.w.) migrated from Makkah to Madinah, the first thing he did was build a community centre—a masjid. The masjid was not only for prayers but also for other activities to engage the community in that which is productive, good and pleasing to Allah (s.w.t.).

Number three you need to get in touch with me inshā'Allāh as well as the Aware Academy. *Alḥamdulillāh*, we have counsellors here in Malaysia who are certified coaches that can help you with addictive sins of that nature *inshā'Allāh.*

Number four and the most important solution is to have a partner that can assist you. You have to develop a support system that will assist you with your struggle so that you can cope *inshā'Allāh*. If you want to fight your addiction by yourself, then remember this: you are the loser. The Prophet (s.a.w.) said in a hadith:

Narrated Abu Hurayrah:

> The Prophet (s.a.w.) said: A man follows the religion of his friend; so each one should consider whom he makes his friend.
>
> (Sunan Abi Dawud 4833)

A person will always be inclined to follow the religion or the way of life of his friend. Thus, you must have a support system that will always remind you of Allah (s.w.t.). My dear brothers and sisters, good friends are those that when you look at them, they remind you of Allah (s.w.t.). However, without a support system, you will never be able to get rid of your addiction. May Allah (s.w.t.) protect and cleanse us all from any addictive and bad habits. *Āmīn.*

Question 7: The Qur'an told us—***lā taḥzan***—do not be sad. How do we balance between embracing our emotion of sadness and this statement?

Mufti Menk:

Bismillāhirraḥmānirraḥīm.

There was a year in the life of the Prophet Muḥammad (s.a.w.) that was called *'Am al-Ḥuzn*, the Year of Sadness. It was called the Year of Sadness because a few things happened to the Prophet (s.a.w.) during that year such as losing his uncle, losing his wife Khadijah (r.a.), the incident of *Ṭa'if* and so on. However, the sadness that the Prophet Muḥammad (s.a.w.) experienced never went to a degree where it came in conflict with what Allah (s.w.t.) had ordained.

It is a common and normal human trait to be happy and sad. However, when our sadness takes us to a level where we become so engrossed in it, it will unplug us from reality. It will perhaps make us distant from our Maker Allah (s.w.t.). It will make us slide into depression. It will take us to a point where we are losing our life.

Thus, do not forget; no matter what loss it was, Allah (s.w.t.) has already developed for us a coping mechanism known as *ṣabr.* Remember as well that we will be rewarded when we endure the tests given by Allah (s.w.t.).

When the Prophet (s.a.w.) lost his son Ibrahim (r.a.), tears were shed. The Prophet's eyes were filled with tears and he (s.a.w.) said إِنَّهَا رَحْمَةٌ—that tears are a sign of mercy.

Narrated Anas bin Malik:

> We went with Allah's Messenger (s.a.w.) to the blacksmith Abu Saif, and he was the husband of the wet-nurse of Ibrahim (the son of the Prophet). Allah's Messenger (s.a.w.) took Ibrahim and kissed him and smelled him and later we entered Abu Saif's house and at that time Ibrahim was in his last breaths, and the eyes of Allah's Messenger (s.a.w.) started shedding tears. 'Abdur-Raḥman bin 'Auf said, "O' Allah's Apostle, even you are weeping!" He said, "O' Ibn 'Auf, this is mercy." Then he wept more and said, "The eyes are shedding tears and the heart is grieved, and we will not say

except what pleases our Lord, O' Ibrahim! Indeed we are grieved by your separation."

(Ṣaḥiḥ al-Bukhari 1303)

Tears are a sign of Allah's mercy.

Tears are the mercy which Allah Almighty places in the hearts of those who **have** mercy.

The Prophet (s.a.w.) mentions in the above hadith that the heart is saddened by the loss of Ibrahim (r.a.) but he will not utter anything that will be displeasing to Allah (s.w.t.). The heart of the Prophet (s.a.w.) was indeed sad and that is a natural sadness felt by a human who has lost his beloved ones. However, what is more important is to remember to not utter that which is displeasing to Allah. Instead, we should say:

... إِنَّ لِلَّهِ مَا أَخَذَ وَلَهُ مَا أَعْطَى وَكُلٌّ شَيْءٍ عِنْدَ اللَّهِ بِأَجَلٍ مُسَمًّى فَلْتَصْبِرْ وَلْتَحْتَسِبْ ...

...to Allah belongs that which He takes and that which He gives, and everything has an appointed time with Allah. Let her be patient and seek reward...

(Sunan an-Nasa'i 1868)

In essence, it is OK to be sad as long as we do not let the sadness get to a level where it begins to affect our entire connection with Allah (s.w.t.) as well as our current life. I know of this one brother who was very young and he had just lost his father. He came to me and said that he could not cope with what had happened. I told him to look at himself, that he was in fact still a teenager. He should still thank Allah as there are others who have lost their father at a younger age than him. Of course, inevitably he has now a huge responsibility. And so, crying about what has happened is completely fine. Shedding tears is not haram. Crying is actually a coping mechanism that is given by Allah (s.w.t.) to us. Shedding tears has a lot of benefits and it is a good thing to cry at times. But then we have to remember to keep going as well.

Let me explain using the example of football. It is the same example I gave to the young brother as well. When one of the top teammates in the football matches gets a red card and is out, everyone will be sad. People will be upset but they will still tell the rest of the team to keep going—to continue to kick the ball and score. There were ten men at the start and it became nine afterwards, but the team can still win if they keep going. Yes, it is a sad moment when you have lost a family member or anyone close. It is OK to feel sad but do not forget that our life is still going on. For the people whom we have lost, we can help them by making *du'a'* for them. We need to continuesly make *du'a'* for them and *inshā'Allāh* it will be a *ṣadaqah jariyah* for them. If we are their child and we do goodness and pray for them—we would then have helped them.

In addition, sadness is OK but as I mentioned not to a point where we are sliding into a place where we are lacking *ṣabr*. I always tell myself to look at those who are struggling across the globe. I had the opportunity to meet some Syrian refugees a few years ago. One of the brothers told me that he had lost absolutely everything. He had to run for his life without anything. He and his wife as well as his daughter had to just run to save their lives. They went on for days like that until they got to the crossing of Turkey. These people are going through so much and here I am complaining about the mosquito in my bedroom which is disturbing me with its sound. To us, the sound of mosquitoes irritates us. However, to some people, it is a sound that they are waiting to hear. That sound to some people would be a gift because at least then they can get some sleep.

Question 8: Instead of a question, I have a small request. I brought my non-Muslim friend who is on the fence to this lecture. I would like to humbly seek Mufti Menk's words to say something that will perhaps convince my friend about Islam.

Dr Muhammad Salah:

May Allah (s.w.t.) open his heart to accept the truth and say the *shahadah*.

Mufti Menk:

Mashā'Allāh, my beloved brother or sister. Firstly, I would like to welcome all those who have yet to be a Muslim. To those who may be considering to be Muslims and to those who are not considering, welcome. Every event has a theme and its topics. While covering the different topics, you would be able to see the teachings of Islam from **within** Islam. One morning, I received a question from someone who was studying Islamic studies in a secular non-Muslim university. He was telling me that what the university was teaching was totally against Islam. However, the lecturer said to him that he must learn it as it is part of the curriculum. The student who asked me this question is a Muslim himself and he was telling me that he knows what Islam is about and it is not what they are teaching. The brother was lost, and he asked me what he should do as they were spreading and teaching falsehood in the name of Islam. I told him that he must raise the topic somehow through channels or find out from other people about what they have done. This is because I do not belong in that university hence, he who is there has to raise the topic somehow. Furthermore, I would not learn Islam from those who are non-Muslims or from those who hate Islam as well as from those who would intentionally teach you the opposite. And so, to come to an Islamic event to witness what Muslims actually do and learn is a really good thing.

There was once in another Islamic event, someone had asked "Why are Muslim terrorists?" I then asked the audience to raise their hand if they were Muslims. Almost everybody raised their hands. I asked the person then whether he felt terrorized in any way while being surrounded by Muslims at the event; and whether he felt safe being at the event. The person replied that he felt very safe actually and I told him that was the answer to his question. The audience are not terrorists—the Muslims are not terrorists.

And so, what I would like to say is that there will always be some inclination within the heart that may say "I need to do this, I need to do that." On the other hand, you would also have *shayṭan* coming to you and saying to you "No, not yet. You don't have to take the *shahadah* yet. Just wait." In essence, the push, the step towards the journey needs to come from us. We are the ones who have to take that step. We are going to be worried about many things but if we are convinced to do something, then start with *bismilllah*.

There is a lot of discipline, contentment and joy that comes with Islam—the true Islam. Perhaps sometimes we have looked at Muslims who are not really practising Islam, and so they may not be able to offer us the true reflection of what Islam is. However, there will definitely be people whom when we look at them, we will say "Oh wow, look at how beautiful they are" and "Wow they are so disciplined." That is Islam, that is the religion of Allah Almighty.

It is up to us to take that step. It is up to us to push ourselves a little bit and take the step. Some might say that they don't know the whole of Islam.

Do you know the five pillars of Islam?

Do you know the six pillars of Iman?

Do you believe in halal and haram?

Do you know the basics?

If yes, then you are ready to say and declare the *shahadah*. What is the *shahadah*?

أَشْهَدُ أَنْ لَا إِلَهَ إِلَّا اللَّهُ وَأَشْهَدُ أَنَّ مُحَمَّدًا رَسُولُ اللَّهِ

I bear witness that there is none worthy of worship except Allah. He is One and has no partner. And I bear witness that Muḥammad is His Servant and Messenger.

The *shahadah* is a declaration that *I bear witness that there is none worthy of worship besides the One who made me, Allah (s.w.t.). And I bear witness that Muḥammad (s.a.w.) is the Messenger of Allah.* Once you have said the *shahadah*, you declare it, and then you believe it in your heart and start practising it. As you learn about Islam, practice more and more of it. You will come to learn the details of how to pray, how to wash up, how to cleanse yourself and so on. You will learn little by little from here and there. Sometimes, people might overwhelm you initially, but this is just because everyone is so excited when someone declares the *shahadah*. People will come to you and tell you to do this and that. You might feel overwhelmed but don't worry. Slowly but surely, you will get to that point as you move at a good pace. Do not let people overwhelm you. It is your journey. There are so many born Muslims and practising Muslims, but they all still have a lot of room for improvement; there are so many things they too have not yet done.

Wael Ibrahim:

The bottom line my dear brothers and sisters is to not delay that decision.

Mufti Menk:

Yes, do not delay the decision because you don't know if you are going to walk out today and go home. I have had the opportunity to study a lot of religions, and with all due respect to all the religions—I am a Muslim because I find Islam the true religion. It is outstanding. It definitely has a lot that outshines everything else. That is why I am a Muslim. I might have been born as a Muslim, but later I reiterated and reconfirmed after studying. And so, I realised that I am so glad and blessed to have been born as a Muslim as I studied the religion. On the other hand, some people have not studied about the religion and so they do not know much about it. There are even some people who are born as Muslims and have not looked closely to the religion. Consequently, they begin to have doubts and they dilly-dally as well. Let me tell you the answers to your doubt. Islam has the answer to all your questions. You just have to get the answers from the right sources.

What do you think will happen when we delay our decisions? You might be thinking that it is OK and you can do it the next day but what if you are not guaranteed for tomorrow? It is *shayṭan* who just wants you to delay.

When you declare the *shahadah*, it is OK if you do not want to publically announce it. The announcement can be within your circles first. Slowly but surely *inshā'Allāh* you will come to a point where you will announce to all—when you are more prepared. However, ideally, you should still let your parents and close friends know. Tell them that this is the beautiful path you have chosen and that you are going to show to people around you that it is going to be an amazing journey.

A brother I knew declared hi *shahadah* without letting his parents know. After becoming a Muslim, *subḥānAllāh* he quit his bad habits—smoking, drugs and so on. The brother ended up doing many good and wonderful things. He became a kinder son as well. One day his mother asked him, "I noticed a change in you since last year. You have become wonderful. What actually happened last year?" The brother asked his mother whether she was ready to know and hear what his turning point was. He also asked, "You won't be upset when I tell you what happened?" And the mother wondered why she would be upset when her son has become the best version of himself. After asking his mum a few times, the brother told her that he had become a Muslim the year before in August. He told his mother that Islam is a religion that teaches to worship the one Maker alone, Allah. In addition, he mentioned how Islam has good rules and regulations—fulfilling the rights of your spouse, mother, father, neighbours and so on. He also mentioned that Muslims pray five times a day so that they are always connected with God, Allah; Islam teaches as well to connect with the people around you. After listening to her son, the mother said, "If that is the case, then I too want to be a Muslim." The brother told me that he felt guilty because he delayed telling his parents about his decision. I told him to not worry because *alḥamdulillāh* Allah (s.w.t.) brought her back before she went back to Him. In essence, it is a good thing to let people know about your decision and you will sometimes be surprised by their unexpected, beautiful reactions. You might think that everyone will be giving you a problem about your decision but that is not the case. Some might but Allah will help you deal with it as long as you pray to Him and depend on Him. In addition, some of my colleagues in the *da'wah* field are reverts and *subḥānAllāh* they are now scholars and public speakers. Some will ask you to pray for their parents—mother and father—to be Muslim. Next thing you know, they will tell you that *alḥamdulillāh* their parents too have accepted Islam. *Alḥamdulillāh.*

On a side note, I wanted to tell you all about social media and online platforms. The followers that we have online mean nothing—zero. What is truly meaningful is everything about who you **really** are. What is online is predominantly artificial and deceptive. Only a little bit of it is the truth. Most people when they meet the person they have been looking at online in reality, they are always taken aback. Most might say that they look very different and that they have spoiled their face. And you know what it means when they have spoiled their faces. So do not be deceived by the numbers that you see online. Do not be deceived by the number of likes. Do not compare. It does not make you better than anyone else. All the people who follow you will not be able to avail you even the weight of a mustard seed on the Day of Judgement; they cannot. However, the *taqwa* and the closeness you have with Allah (s.w.t.) **will** and that is of the utmost importance.

May Allah (s.w.t.) help us to improve ourselves. *Āmīn.*

Arabic Glossary

1. *Al-baraṣ* : leprosy/leper
2. *Alḥamdulillāh* : Praise be to Allah
3. *Al-istisqa'*: offering prayers for rain
4. *'Am al-Ḥuzn* : Year of Sporrow
5. *Ithar* : selflessness
6. *Allāhu Akbar* : Allah is the Greatest
7. *Al-ujub* : excessive self-admiration
8. *As-salaf* : predecessors
9. *As-sama'*: inhabitants of the heaven
10. *At-tabi'in* : follower
11. *Awliya'*: guardian
12. *Ayah* : verse
13. *Ayatul iktibar* : lesson
14. *Ayatul imtiḥan* : test
15. *Batarul-Haqq* : distain and rejection of the Truth
16. *Bi iznillāh :* with the permission of Allah
17. *Bomoh* : witch doctor (in Malay culture)
18. *Da'wah* : a call to embrace Islam
19. *Din* : religion
20. *Dunya* : worldly
21. *Farḍ*: religious duty commanded by God
22. *Fiṭrah*: natural inclination
23. *Ḥatta uḥibbah* : until Allah loves you
24. *Ḥijrah*: migration
25. *Ḥusnul khatimah* : good ending
26. *Jannah*: Paradise
27. *Jannahtul Firdaus* : The highest level of Paradise
28. *Khamr* : alcohol/wine
29. *Kibr* : pride, arrogant,
30. *Kufr* : disbelief
31. *Mashā'Allāh* : as Allah has willed
32. *Mustajab* : answered or accepted

33. *Nawafil* : optional prayer
34. *Qiyamah* : The Day of Judgement
35. *Rak'ah*: a single iteration of prescribed movements and supplications performed by Muslims as part of the prescribed obligatory prayer known as *ṣalah*
36. *riḍa* : contentment
37. *Ṣabr*: patience
38. *Ṣadaqah* : charity
39. *Ṣaḥabi* : companions
40. *Ṣalah* : prayer
41. *Shahadah*: Islamic declaration of faith
42. *Shayṭan*: devil
43. *Shirk* : polytheism
44. *Sirah* : life of Prophet Muḥammad (s.a.w.)
45. *SubḥānAllāh* : Glory be to Allah
46. *Ṭaghut* : whoever that is worshipped other than Allah
47. *Taḥajjud*: supplementary night prayer
48. Ṭaharah : cleanliness or purification
49. *Taqwa* : piety
50. *Tawḥid* : unification of Allah
51. *Ṭuma'ninah* : tranquility
52. *Ummah*: community
53. *Walā 'a'ūdhubillāh* : I seek refuge in Allah
54. *Wuḍu'*: ablution
55. *Zakat*: almsgiving
56. *Zina* : illicit sexual relations

www.ingramcontent.com/pod-product-compliance
Lightning Source LLC
LaVergne TN
LVHW061630070526
838199LV00071B/6631
* 9 7 8 9 6 7 2 8 4 4 3 2 7 *